Grading Students' Classroom Writing

Issues and Strategies

P9-DFG-301

Bruce W. Speck

ASHE-ERIC Higher Education Report Volume 27, Number 3

Prepared by

ERIC Clearinghouse on Higher Education
The George Washington University
URL: www.eriche.org

In cooperation with

Saint Peter's University Library
Withdrawn

Association for the Study of Higher Education
URL: http://www.tiger.coe.missouri.edu/~ashe

Published by

Graduate School of Education and Human Development
The George Washington University
URL: www.gwu.edu

Adrianna J. Kezar, Series Editor

Cite as

Speck, B. W. (2000). *Grading Students' Classroom Writing: Issues and Strategies*. ASHE-ERIC Higher Education Report (Vol. 27, No. 3). Washington, DC: The George Washington University, Graduate School of Education and Human Development.

Library of Congress Catalog Card Number
ISSN 0884-0040
ISBN 1-878380-91-5

Managing Editor: Lynne J. Scott
Manuscript Editor: Barbara M. Fishel
Cover Design by Michael David Brown, Inc., The Red Door Gallery, Rockport, ME

The ERIC Clearinghouse on Higher Education invites individuals to submit proposals for writing monographs for the *ASHE-ERIC Higher Education Report* series. Proposals must include:

1. A detailed manuscript proposal of not more than five pages.
2. A chapter-by-chapter outline.
3. A 75-word summary to be used by several review committees for the initial screening and rating of each proposal.
4. A vita and a writing sample.

ERIC Clearinghouse on Higher Education
Graduate School of Education and Human Development
The George Washington University
One Dupont Circle, Suite 630
Washington, DC 20036-1183

The mission of the ERIC system is to improve American education by increasing and facilitating the use of educational research and information on practice in the activities of learning, teaching, educational decision making, and research, wherever and whenever these activities take place.

This publication was prepared partially with funding from the Office of Educational Research and Improvement, U.S. Department of Education, under contract no. ED-99-00-0036. The opinions expressed in this report do not necessarily reflect the positions or policies of OERI or the Department.

EXECUTIVE SUMMARY

"How can I grade students' writing?" is a perennial question professors ask, regardless of their discipline. While a great deal of literature about grading classroom writing is available to professors (Speck, 1998a), that literature is scattered throughout a variety of sources. The purpose of *Grading Students' Classroom Writing: Issues and Strategies* is to synthesize major issues in the literature to make it accessible to professors throughout the disciplines. Thus, *Grading Students' Classroom Writing* discusses the relation of the writing process to the grading process, ways to construct effective writing assignments, theoretical issues in grading related to fairness and professional judgment, ways to include students in the assessment of writing, and guidelines professors can use to provide effective feedback for students to revise their writing. It does not focus on discipline-specific criteria for grading students' writing, because each discipline has its own norms and conventions. Professors need to communicate these norms and conventions to students to effectively and fairly grade students' writing.

Why Is It Important to Integrate Grading Into the Writing Process?

The writing process is recursive and includes various stages of revision. In integrating grading into the writing process, professors must consider the relationship between the grading process and a grade. The *grading process* results in a *grade,* the final evaluation professors give either to an individual assignment or to a series of assignments that included grades for individual writing assignments within the series. The grade is one part of the grading process, not the focus of the process. Indeed, the grading process extends from the development of a writing assignment to the administration of a final grade. When the grade is abstracted from the grading process, students may be left wondering how a grade was derived, professors may be put in the awkward position of explaining and defending a grade after the fact, and evaluation may be severed from the process of writing.

Nevertheless, integrating grading and the writing process is not without difficulties, including tension between the professor's roles as mentor and judge. The dual roles of mentor and judge raise ethical issues about the grading process and the grade and, in some quarters, undercut the writing process in favor of the grade. Such undercutting is unfortunate because the writing process can help students learn not only how to approach a writing task effectively but also how to evaluate their own and their peers' writing.

Why Do Professors Need to Construct Effective Writing Assignments?

Because the writing assignment specifies what students are expected to do and how students' written products will be evaluated, the writing assignment should include necessary information about audience and purpose, the two pillars of writing. The writing assignment also is the appropriate occasion for discussing discipline-specific norms and conventions for writing. Writing assignments, like most written products, should go through a process that includes peer review, so professors can enlist colleagues and students to critique writing assignments before the assignments are formally introduced.

How Can Professors Ensure That Their Professional Judgments Are Fair?

Although answers to the question of fairness are often discussed in terms of reliability and validity, the application of statistical requirements for reliability and validity are probably impractical in grading classroom writing. Grading methods that include the use of a rubric or some other tangible expression of grading criteria can promote greater fairness in grading, however (Anderson & Speck, 1998). Nevertheless, fairness in classroom assessment is complicated by a variety of issues (Allison, Bryant, & Hourigan, 1997; White, Lutz, & Kamusikiri, 1996; Zak & Weaver, 1998). In fact, fairness is inextricably linked with professional judgment, because the professor is the grading authority in the classroom. Thus, professors need to be sensitive to their responsibility for fairness when they grade students' papers.

How Can Professors Use Their Authority to Promote Students' Learning?

A powerful way to promote students' learning is to involve them in the grading process. To do so, professors should consider training students to function effectively as peer reviewers, modeling for them the integration of formal, subject matter, and teaching authority into the grading process so that students have examples of professional evaluators they can emulate when they serve as peer reviewers. When students are given the opportunity to function as professionals in the classroom, they can learn how to make informed decisions about writing quality, a task many students will be required to do in their vocations in nonacademic settings. Students' involvement also includes self-assessments.

How Can the Professor Help Students to Learn How to Respond Effectively to Writing?

Providing effective feedback to students will help them learn to revise their writing. Unfortunately, the literature on professors' feedback to students' writing includes numerous examples of how *not* to provide feedback. Three common inappropriate responses are cryptic responses, negative responses, and too much response. These forms of response are predicated on views of grading that are not commensurate with the writing process, primarily because they focus on errors. Fortunately, negative examples can serve a cautionary note, suggesting that professors need to learn how to provide effective feedback. Professors can take a step toward providing useful feedback by recognizing the perils they face when they read students' writing. When professors are sensitive to those perils, they can take a more cautious and more positive approach to reading and responding to students' writing. In particular, professors can provide written comments on students' writing by creating a dialogue when writing responses, pointing out successful writing, refraining from making unprofessional comments, summarizing the gist of marginal comments at the end of a paper, giving students options for revising the paper, writing comments that model good writing, and deferring the assignment of a grade as long as possible. Positive, well written responses perfect the art of providing effective feedback to students and serve as models of desirable writing.

What Support Is Available to Help Professors Effectively Grade Students' Writing?

Effective grading of students' writing is hard work that requires a great deal of time and a commitment to reading the literature on grading classroom writing. Without administrative support, including appropriate class sizes and teaching loads, professors need to consider just how much time and energy they should devote to promoting the intertwining of the writing and grading processes. To the extent that professors do elect to use these intertwining processes, they might consider establishing a plan to integrate the processes in their classes over an extended period of time and to consult the literature on the grading of classroom writing for detailed information about effectively promoting the writing and grading processes.

CONTENTS

Foreword ix
Acknowledgments xiii

The Writing Process and Grading Students' Writing 1
The Writing Process 1
Problems Fitting Evaluation With the Writing Process 3
Issues Related to the Grading Process 5
Marrying the Writing and Grading Processes 8

Constructing Writing Assignments 11
Determining Purpose and Audience 11
Determining and Specifying What Is Essential and What Is Optional 18
Determining What Standards Will Be Used to Evaluate Students' Written Responses to the Assignment 21
Critiquing Writing Assignments 23
Conclusion 26

Fairness and Professional Judgment 27
Theoretical Issues Related to Reliability, Validity, Fairness, and Professional Judgment 27
Grading Methods 31
Conclusion 44

Including Students in the Assessment of Writing 45
Professorial Authorities 45
Cheating 47
Preparing Students to Make Informed Decisions About the Quality of Writing 51
Ways to Include Students in the Grading Process 52
Conclusion 60

Providing Feedback for Revision: Reading and Responding to Students' Writing 61
Common Misperceptions About Feedback 61
Why Professors Might Have Difficulties Providing Effective Feedback 65
How Professors Can Provide Useful Feedback 70
Conclusion 75

Conclusion and Recommendations 77

Appendix: Example of a Student's Paper With Effective Written Comments 81

References 85
Index 99

ASHE-ERIC Higher Education Reports **103**
Advisory Board 105
Consulting Editors 107
Review Panel 111
Recent Titles 115
Order Form 119

FOREWORD

Many individuals and organizations, particularly among the public sector, have expressed concern about the quality of teaching in colleges and universities. Graduate education as well has recently come under scrutiny. What are doctoral students learning that will help them to be better teachers? What learning theories do they review in the course of their studies? What skills and competencies are they developing? Are they obtaining substantial experiences as apprentice teachers? These questions are important. The results of various studies on graduate education show that students receive little, if any, training in pedagogy, including learning about theory, developing skills, or actually teaching in a classroom. The most common experience graduate students have is as a teaching assistant. Graduate students and, later, assistant professors often flounder without appropriate theoretical or practical knowledge.

Several movements around the country, however, suggest that this situation is changing. A comprehensive study by the University of Washington is examining ways to transform graduate education. Programs such as the Preparing Future Faculty project sponsored by the Council for Graduate Schools and the Association of American Colleges and Universities focus on working with campuses to develop model programs for teaching graduate students not only about instruction, but also about the various aspects of a faculty role—service, involvement in governance, and learning more about the enterprise of higher education.

Moreover, concerns have been raised about the ability of existing faculty, many of whom were not formally trained, to teach. Centers for teaching excellence are being created across the country with the intent of providing tools and techniques to faculty who want to improve their teaching abilities and the learning of students.

Although programs for graduate students and centers for faculty development are being created, resources on teaching are needed for the curricula of these programs. Many general books about teaching are available, among them *The Aims of College Teaching* by Kenneth Eble, *Becoming a Critically Reflective Teacher* by Stephen Brookfield, *The Courage to Teach* by Parker Palmer, and *Mastering the Techniques of Teaching* by Joseph Lowman, yet fewer resources are available that provide guidance on specific issues of teaching. One outstanding exception is *Education for Judgment: The Artistry of*

Discussion Leadership by Roland Christensen, David Garvin, and Ann Sweet.

Yet many aspects of the teaching and learning processes need specific advice and strategies because they can be fraught with difficulty. Teaching students to write well and grading what they have written are two complex processes that even expert teachers do not always do well. Therefore, *Grading Students' Classroom Writing: Issues and Strategies* by Bruce W. Speck is an important addition to the literature on teaching and learning. Dr. Speck has had many years of experience with this issue as associate vice chancellor for academic affairs at The University of North Carolina at Pembroke and earlier as acting director of the Center for Academic Excellence at The University of Memphis. These positions, as well as experience as coordinator of the Writing-Across-the-Curriculum program at Memphis, resulted in efforts to help faculty and graduate students improve teaching.

Grading Students' Classroom Writing provides detailed and complex guidance and the necessary techniques for grading writing. It reviews issues of fairness, reliability and validity, peer grading and evaluation, cheating, and effective feedback, maintaining a developmental approach to improving students' writing. Throughout, grading is seen as a process, not a product. The grading process is integral to students' learning, not just an exercise in registering ability or merit. *Grading Students' Classroom Writing* is also sensitive to disciplinary differences in grading writing, unlike many resources on teaching, which do not acknowledge the differences among disciplines.

It is exciting to add this monograph to the ASHE-ERIC Higher Education Report series. I hope you will review our catalog, which lists more than 30 different monographs on teaching and learning. Some of the other monographs on teaching and learning can help supplement your program for graduate students or add to resources for your center for teaching excellence: *Creating Learning Centered Classrooms* by Frances Stage, Patricia Muller, Jillian Kinzie, and Ada Simmons; *The Powerful Potential of Learning Communities* by Oscar Lenning and Larry Ebbers; *Active Learning* by Charles Bonwell and James Eison; *Cooperative Learning* by David Johnson, Roger Johnson, and Karl Smith; *Critical Thinking* by Joanne Kurfiss; *Enacting Diverse Learning Environments* by Sylvia Hurtdao, Jeff Milem, Alma Clayton-Pedersen, and

Walter Allen; and *Experiential Learning in Higher Education* by Jeffrey Cantor. These titles are just a sample of the rich resources available through ASHE-ERIC that can enhance your efforts to improve the teaching and learning process on your campus. Learning is the central mission of higher education institutions, and it is critical that important resources such as Bruce Speck's *Grading Students' Classroom Writing* continue to be written, synthesizing the best practices from research on teaching and learning.

Adrianna J. Kezar
Series Editor,
Assistant Professor of Higher Education, and
Director, ERIC Clearinghouse on Higher Education

ACKNOWLEDGMENTS

I greatly appreciate the support of Dr. Sidney A. McPhee, vice chancellor for academic affairs and strategic planning at the Tennessee Board of Regents. I also appreciate the insights of five anonymous reviewers who pointed out ways to improve the manuscript; I have incorporated their suggested revisions whenever possible. In addition, my family was very supportive during the writing process for this monograph. In particular, I wish to thank my daughter Heidi, who read the book in manuscript form and provided helpful comments for making revisions.

THE WRITING PROCESS AND GRADING STUDENTS' WRITING

In the teaching of writing, writing and grading were each seen traditionally as one-step activities. The student created a text to fulfill an assignment, and the professor examined a finished text to grade it. Professors assumed that students knew how to satisfy the requirements for a writing assignment and that grading students' written products entailed rendering a professional judgment based on canons of correctness, disciplinary conventions, and aesthetic principles—all of which were accepted by professionals in a discipline. Any process related to writing and grading was either assumed to be understood or was beyond question, because writing was based on innate abilities and grading was based on professional judgment.

These long-held assumptions about the transparency of writing and grading were questioned in the 1960s when open enrollment policies at U. S. universities made higher education available to students who had not received traditional preparation for successful participation in higher education. Professors too were unprepared for the writing these nontraditional students offered as their efforts at fulfilling writing assignments. Out of the questions that were raised about writing came landmark studies, including Mina Shaughnessy's *Errors and Expectations* (1977), which explained how "basic" writers, those students who wrote prose that professors could not decipher because it contained what appeared to be exotic errors, could be helped to become card-carrying members of the academic writing community; studies by Linda Flower and John Hayes, which explained the cognitive processes writers use when they write; works by Peter Elbow, which provided teachers with advice about how to promote a student-centered writing process in the classroom; and a host of books and articles about what has come to be known as "the writing process."

The Writing Process

Writing, as it turns out, is not a one-shot affair, given literature on the creation of literary works (Bendixen, 1986; Bonetti, 1988; Leonard, Wharton, Davis, & Harris, 1994), business and technical documents (Bazerman, 1983; Dautermann, 1993; Odell & Goswami, 1985; Smart, 1993), and scholarly works (Anson, Brady, & Larson, 1993; Ashton-Jones & Thomas, 1990; Brodkey, 1987). The substantial literature on journal and book publishing, and grant agency peer review is another rich source of information about the writing process in various professional contexts (Speck, 1993). This is not to say that students don't continue to write papers the night before they are due; rather, it is to say that the best way to approach a writing task is by following a recursive process that includes exploring the various dimensions of a topic, conducting research about the topic to include various kinds of primary and secondary research methods, writing some sort of draft, thinking about the topic some more, continuing to conduct research, writing some more, talking with peers about the shape the paper is taking, writing some more, asking the professor for insight into the relationship between the writing assignment and the individual writing task being performed, shaping a draft that peers can review, examining the validity of peer reviewers' comments and suggestions for revision, revising the draft (generally more than one time), participating in a student-teacher conference, perhaps doing more research, revising by honing in on the thesis, polishing a "final" draft for editorial review, making editorial changes to the draft, and submitting it for a grade.

The problem with using a list to describe the writing process is that a list is just that—a list of sequential events. The recursive writing process writing theorists describe is much messier than the above list suggests. Students grope toward their topic, unsure of what exactly they want or need to say about it; chase a topic down a blind alley and then retrace their steps, reconceptualizing their topic as they synthesize information; write a draft that helps them think through the various strands of information they are trying to weave together into a tapestry; take a walk and let what they're trying to create simmer and brew; mix different ingredients into the concoction they are creating; and so forth. (And the mixed metaphors are emblematic of the writing process as the writer's viewpoint shifts from one perspective to another in a series of efforts to create a cohesive document.) It is not the case that writers follow a clean, linear line from generating a topic to editing final copy. Rather, the writing process is like a scientific experiment, with chemicals combined in different proportions and types in many, many iterations and with adjustments to the procedure as the experiment progresses, until the appropriate chemicals produce the desired result.

I use chemistry as an analogy because one meaning of the word *chemistry* is a certain something that cannot be quantified; things just click. This meaning can be applied to the writing process. Along the winding and recursive writing path that circles back upon itself, things just click, and the parts of a writing project come together into a cohesive product. To say "things just click," however, is not to minimize the agonizing effort that writers exert to enjoy the clicking they experience during the writing process. Writing is hard work over an extended period of time, not a one-shot effort.

Studies of the writing process lead to questions about how writing should be taught and evaluated. If writing is a process, then shouldn't professors provide students with opportunities to revise their written work with the goal of making that work the best possible? In other words, shouldn't a major pedagogical purpose of writing instruction—in any discipline—be to teach students how to be successful writers in that particular discipline? The new focus on writing instruction as a responsibility all professors share spawned the writing-across-the-curriculum movement and a literature about integrating the process approach to writing into the academic disciplines (Anson, Schwiebert, & Williamson, 1993). In addition, a literature developed that included all kinds of ideas about how professors can make evaluation a process that fits with the process approach to writing (Speck, 1998a), including examples of assessing classroom writing (Angelo & Cross, 1993; Banta, Lund, Black, & Oblander, 1996). The problems of fitting the evaluation process with the writing process, however, have been difficult to solve for three reasons.

If writing is a process, then shouldn't professors provide students with opportunities to revise their written work with the goal of making that work the best possible?

Problems Fitting Evaluation With the Writing Process

The first problem is that professors who have accepted the writing process as a way to help students learn to write may not be much interested in evaluating final products. The focus for these professors is the process, not the product. In fact, they may want to leave the process open ended, believing that the goal of writing pedagogy is to provide the maximum opportunity for students to use the process. Professors who hold to this position might state their view as "process, not product," perhaps in reaction to the traditional view of product, not process. Because grading traditionally was attached to the final product, the purpose of the process is not only to deemphasize final products, but also to call into question final grades. Thus, grades becomes an enemy of the process approach to writing (Bleich, 1992; Blinderman, 1970; Duke, 1980; Winterowd, 1971).

Second, the terminology of evaluation is extremely unstable (Speck, 1998c). What exactly do professors mean when they say they have graded a student's writing? Have the professors marked it, evaluated it, assessed it, and put a grade on it? Or have they simply put an abstract mark, that is, A, B, C, D, or F, on the paper? (Speck & Jones, 1998). What are the functions of marginal and terminal comments—the written feedback professors give in the margins and at the end of a student's paper—when they are used in conjunction with a final grade? And what is the relationship between a "final" grade on one writing assignment and a "final" grade on another writing assignment? Do such grades necessarily show growth in a student's writing ability? What exactly does *the* final grade say about a student's writing ability?

Third, literature on the classroom grading of students' writing raises a number of political, cultural, and ethical questions about grading (see, e.g., Bloom, 1997; Marshall, 1997; J. Sommers, Black, Daiker, & Stygall, 1993; White, Lutz, & Kamusikiri, 1996). What role do gender and race play in grading? (Ballard & Clanchy, 1991; Barnes, 1990; E. Flynn, 1989; J. Flynn, 1989; Gabriel, 1990; Haswell & Tedesco, 1991; Stygall, Black, Daiker, & Sommers, 1994). Isn't the professor in an ethical dilemma when he or she assumes the role of tutor, one who shepherds students through the writing process, and then assumes the role of grader, one who, ironically, makes final judgments about students' written products or, perhaps worse, their ability to use the writing process effectively? Is it ethical for the professor to assume both roles? (Belanger, 1985; Ede, 1980). What about the role of preparing professors to grade students' writing? Are professors given adequate training in preparation for carrying out their classroom duties related to assessing students' writing? Can they demonstrate that their grades are valid and reliable? That is, can professors show that the criteria they say they use to give grades to students are indeed the criteria they do use? Can professors show that the criteria they use to grade the writing student S did for assignment P was the criteria they used to grade all other students' writing for assignment P? Further, can professors show that the criteria they used to help students write during the writing process are the same criteria they used to grade the written products students produced as a result of the process? (The humbling answer to such questions is, in general, "no." See Blok, 1985; Bowman, 1973; Charnley, 1978; Dulek & Shelby, 1981; Garrison, 1979; Rachal, 1984; Sneed, 1986; Wilkinson, 1979.)

Issues Related to the Grading Process

The first question that must be answered is the one about terminology, and two things need to be said in answering that question. First, whether the word *evaluation, assessment,* or *grading* is used, these terms must be understood to encompass a process that includes multiple steps and should not be confined to whatever professors do to a final draft of a student's writing. In accordance with the best research on composition theory, classroom evaluation, assessment, and grading should become intertwined with the writing process. (For the purposes of not repeating the trio of terms throughout this book, the words *evaluating, assessing,* and *grading* will be used interchangeably to encompass the entire process of evaluating students' writing.) *Grading* is perhaps the most common term used to refer to both the process of evaluating students' writing and the product of that process, a grade. In this monograph, however, *grading* and *grade* are distinct terms. While *grading,* along with *assessing* and *evaluating,* refers to the integration of the process of writing with the process of providing insights and judgments about students' writing, *grade* refers to the administrative product of grading, the grade, not only for individual assignments but also for the cumulative grade derived from adding the grades on individual assignments.

Before continuing this discussion on the terms used to describe grading, two points need to be made. First, a professor should distinguish between giving feedback to students about their writing and assigning a grade to the writing. The purpose of feedback is to help students improve their writing and to praise what students do well. Thus, the purpose of giving feedback is to promote the writing process, and the professor can fulfill that purpose without giving a grade. Second, the purpose of giving a grade, however, is to fulfill administrative requirements, and professors make an enormous assumption when they believe that a grade alone tells students very much about the quality of their writing. In fact, attaching grades to students' writing does not necessarily promote the writing process. I suggest, therefore, that professors make a clear distinction between their role as a reader of students' writing who gives helpful feedback so that students can revise their writing and their role as a grader. (Readers interested in a discussion of the distinctions among terms used to characterize grading should see Speck & Jones, 1998.) Now we can return to the problem of grading terminology.

The following comments about *assessment* pertain to whatever term one uses to name the process professors should use in grading, evaluating, or assessing students' writing:

> *An* assessment *may occur formally or informally whenever one person seeks and interprets information about another person. An "assessment of writing" occurs when a teacher, evaluator, or researcher obtains information about a student's abilities in writing. This information may be gathered in classrooms through observations, class assignments, or formal tests. Assessment information may be gathered without tests or without any kind of measurement that implies fixed standards. Assessment procedures do not require the comparison and ranking of students, or the attaching of a letter or number score to the performance. Assessments can be descriptive without being evaluative. In everyday usage, however, the two terms—assessment and evaluation—tend to be synonymous.* (Ruth & Murphy, 1988, p. 6)

Ruth and Murphy are saying three things about assessment. First, assessment takes many forms, including professional observations. A complete assessment picture, it appears, would include various types of assessments over time. While Ruth and Murphy do not say that a grade is the culmination of these various assessments, it is fair to note that that is exactly what a grade is, and it is also fair to note that a grade seems to be an extremely limited description of all those assessments. Grades, then, are containers that include all kinds of information, but that information may be known only to the professor, maybe to the student as well, but probably not to other interested parties who try to interpret grades—parents, spouses, department chairs, deans, provosts, college and university presidents, legislators, testing agencies, and so forth. A grade, therefore, has significant limitations in providing content information about writing performance, and those limitations might very well hinder students from understanding what a grade means in a particular context unless that grade is interpreted by the professor giving the grade. Professors need to provide each student with the content they are dropping into the grade container, so that when the container is full the student has adequate information to give meaning to the grade. (Different grades may come in different sizes, so a C container may be larger than an A container and may be quite full of content.)

Second, Ruth and Murphy say that assessment procedures need not be based on standard notions of ranking students. This idea, of course, is quite contrary to admission practices at many colleges and university. High schools even recognize the necessity of ranking when they provide students with class rank their senior year so that students can inform institutions of higher education of their standing in a class of 1,200 or whatever the number of members in a senior class. Graduate schools are keenly interested in ranking and GPA. Businesses also seem anxious to know a student's numerical status in the graduation line that extends from the summas to the relieved. Is it useful or practical, then, to consider Ruth and Murphy's statement that assessment does not need to include ranking?

For the purposes of this monograph, the philosophy and politics of ranking through grading is not the focal point. Theoretically, students do not need to be ranked when they are awarded grades (Elbow, 1993), but the practice of ranking is deeply ingrained in higher education. The point that grading does not need to include ranking is worth considering in the classroom grading of students' writing, however. How can professors give grades without ranking, especially since grades (or numerical scores) are embedded in a hierarchy of values? Is it possible for professors to award grades without ranking students? When a professor reads a batch of students' papers, can the professor keep from comparing students with each other and thereby setting up a putative ranking system, however inchoate it is? Is it the case that any batch of student papers will by statistical necessity have some papers that are better in comparison with other papers? If professors don't succumb to the ranking syndrome, what are they doing when they ultimately give a grade to a student's writing? What standard are they using to determine how to award grades, and what is the basis for the standard? Is a student's personal growth an adequate measure for grading, and if it is, how is such growth measured? (Bishop, 1989; A. M. Cohen, 1973; Denman, 1978; Freedman & Pringle, 1980; Keech, 1982; Knoblauch & Brannon, 1984; Metzger, 1978). Is it appropriate to compare one student's growth in writing with another student's? If not, is a standardized measure of growth available? Whether a professor does or does not believe in ranking students, issues related to ranking persist as stubborn concerns that do not yield easily to superficial answers about measuring students' writing ability.

Third, Ruth and Murphy note that assessment can be descriptive and does not have to result in a score of some sort. While this notion is certainly true of certain forms of assessment, such as oral feedback a professor gives to students about their writing during a writing conference, ultimately, assessment is reduced to a grade in the vast majority of institutions of higher education. In fact, Ruth and Murphy pose questions about the relationship between grading as a process and the awarding of a grade, especially at the end of the process. How do the two fit together? How can a professor's classroom observations about a student's writing abilities be translated into something that can be measured and ultimately graded? Certainly, some have advocated the abolition of grades, believing that the judgments a professor makes cannot be translated into a grade. They may be correct, but not many people have been convinced that professors should cease to give grades, and as the end of a term approaches with menacing speed, professors become increasingly aware of their contractual obligations to present completed grade rosters to the registrar—or else! Grades may be a great evil, but they are a mandated evil by most of the powers that be. The purpose of this monograph is not to point out all the evils—real and supposed—that grades engender. Rather, the purpose of this monograph is to provide professors with help in determining how to marry the process approach to writing with a process approach to grading.

The purpose of this monograph is to provide professors with help in determining how to marry the process approach to writing with a process approach to grading.

Marrying the Writing and Grading Processes

To marry the two process approaches, professors need to match assessment practices with particular points in the writing process. It really is not helpful to suggest in some vague way that the writing process should be shot through with the assessment process. The obvious response to such an assertion is, What points of the writing process should assessment aim for? Three convenient points are the beginning, the middle, and the end, and while the middle "point" may seem a bit broad, it, too, can be refined to include specific points during the middle process.

In the following sections, the beginning refers to the writing assignment and includes assessment standards and instruments introduced at the outset of the assignment. The middle refers to the bulk of time the students will spend working to satisfy the requirements of the writing assessment. The majority of assessment techniques are used during the middle point. The end refers to the point where the professor sums up the process into a grade. The end point for each piece of writing a student produces generally has another end: the cumulative grade for all the writing the student produces in the class. It is to the beginning, middle, and end points that we now turn.

CONSTRUCTING WRITING ASSIGNMENTS

The writing assignment is the beginning point for assessing students' writing, because the writing assignment is the professor's explanation of what students are required to write to meet the evaluator's/professor's expectations. "Lackluster assignment construction contributes greatly to students' difficulties in completing assignments to their own satisfaction and that of their professors. Assignment construction also affects grading ease and reliability" (Hobson, 1998, p. 52). The problem most professors face in constructing writing assignments is that professors have not been taught how to evaluate such assignments and thus do not have a clear idea of how to satisfy guidelines for creating effective writing assignments. So what are the guidelines for evaluating writing assignments? I suggest three. First, determine purpose and audience. Second, determine what is essential and what is optional. Third, determine what standards will be used to evaluate students' written response to the assignment.

Determining Purpose and Audience

The two pillars of writing—whether teaching it or actually writing—are purpose and audience. What is the purpose for a particular assignment? Who is (are) the audience(s)?

Purpose

By purpose, I do not mean the administrative purpose of providing an opportunity for grading. If the primary purpose for writing assignments is the grading of the writing generated by an assignment, then administrative purposes have superseded educational purposes. Rather, the primary purpose for any writing assignment is to provide students with the opportunity to practice their writing skills so as to further develop those skills. Grading the "final" product of those skills may or may not motivate students to continue writing and may or may not give students satisfactory responses to their writing. Quite frankly, a grade can be ambiguous and of little value in promoting effective writing. So the educative purpose should be the focal point when we talk about the purpose of a writing assignment.

One way to think about the purposes of a writing assignment is to identify two phases of writing: writing to learn and writing to inform. When students write to learn, they explore topics through writing to find out what to say about a topic. Students write so that they can learn. When students have informed themselves about a topic by writing about the topic, they can write to inform others about the topic. In an extended writing assignment, writing to learn logically precedes writing to inform. Thus, students engage in a variety of drafts to explore or learn about a topic and then, at some point in the drafting process, take what they have learned and frame it for their audience. But the extended writing assignment is not the only way to use writing to learn and to inform. The professor can use writing to find out what students know or have learned at a particular point. A professor could ask students during class to summarize an idea from an assigned reading to determine whether the class as a whole can articulate the idea. Students can be grouped into threes and asked to write one summary. Then each group can read aloud its summary to the class. The professor can then determine whether the class as a whole understood the idea. (The professor does not have to collect, read, or grade the writing students do to summarize the idea. In fact, professors do not have the obligation to read, comment on, and grade all the writing students do for a class. Some writing assignments merely have the function of helping students think aloud or demonstrating their level of understanding about a particular idea.)

Given this overview of writing to learn and writing to inform, what, then, are the possible purposes of writing assignments? Writing assignments generally have multiple purposes (Walvoord, 1986), including providing students with opportunities to learn and to practice using new forms (e.g., laboratory reports, the research paper in a particular discipline, PowerPoint presentations, a type of poetry such as sonnets, book reviews, and interviews), to build on existing skills (e.g., using the ability to write a succinct one-page request memo to create an executive summary, using the ability to analyze an issue in microeconomics to then analyze an issue in macroeconomics, using the ability to explore tonal relationship in triadic chords to describe relationships in more complex chordal structures), and to experiment (e.g., using new vocabulary, creating longer and more complex sentences, exploring concepts that require higher levels of thinking).

Certainly, a writing assignment could include more than one of those purposes. For instance, an assignment could ask students to practice a new form, such as a memo, and create a succinct message using specific engineering terms.

In most cases, however, the more an assignment asks students to exert themselves in a variety of directions, the more "errors" will be evident. For instance, when students try out new vocabulary, they often use new words in stilted ways, not being familiar with the nuances of the vocabulary. The professor, then, has to decide what the purpose is of asking students to incorporate new words into an assignment. If the reason is to give students practice in using the vocabulary, then, even if students' usage is incorrect, the professor may not want to penalize students for practicing usage. Again, if one of the purposes of the assignment is to help students learn a new form, professors may not want to penalize students for making errors, but rather point out the errors and provide opportunities for students to master the form. Thus, one purpose of writing assignments, at least in the early stages of teaching new information, is to give students opportunities to practice using the new information without the threat of penalties. At the same time, professors can give students the assurance that continual practice using the new information will be evaluated more thoroughly later.

Often, one purpose of a writing assignment is to induct students into disciplinary writing. Commonly, research papers in a particular discipline require a particular format. Although the professor should acknowledge that no format has a corner on the entire research paper market, thus admitting the variability of forms and the lack of absolute standards regarding format, the professor also should note that those who endorse disciplinary standards judge a piece of writing according to those standards. An example is the IMRAD format for scientific articles (Introduction, Methods, Results, And Discussion), which specifies generic headings. A scientific article written in IMRAD format will have the major headings Introduction, Methods, Results, and Discussion. The audience for a paper that follows IMRAD format will expect those generic headings. Headings for other scientific works, however, such as a review article, are content specific. In academic disciplines in the humanities, by contrast, articles may be narratives and may not even have headings.

Another disciplinary difference is format for citations. Just because a discipline requires American Psychological Association (APA) format should not obscure the point that APA format is only one among many, including University of Chicago (which endorses two styles for citations), Modern

Language Association, Associated Press, Government Printing Office, and so on. Students need to recognize that professors from various disciplines may call upon them to use a number of formats. Professors can help students see that any one format is merely a host of bundled conventions instead of an absolute standard of correctness and virtue.

Making standards absolute is dangerous not only because disciplines vary a great deal in what is regarded as appropriate, right, and proper writing, but also because good writing in one discipline is not necessarily good writing in another. Good writing cannot be defined without reference to a particular context. Good writing "is writing that is perceived to be good" (Raymond, 1982, p. 401). In some disciplines, the use of *I* in certain contexts (e.g., a scientific research article) still has not gained wide acceptance, and good writing in those disciplines generally disallows the use of it. In other disciplines, the use of *I* is considered natural and desirable, and good writing requires the personal involvement that the use of *I* suggests. Thus, the purpose of inducting students into disciplinary ethos as it is expressed in writing should be tempered with the recognition that disciplines allow for different expressions of ethos. Grading the prose of a scientific research article using disciplinary standards for the personal essay (even if the personal essay is written by a scientist about a scientific topic and published in a scientific publication) is a bit of nonsense. Yet professors may continue to instruct students never to use *I* in their writing, even their writing of a research paper in the humanities, when, in fact, examples of articles in philosophy, religion, history, and English journals in which authors use *I* to refer to themselves are readily available to dispute an absolutist approach to disciplinary conventions. If one purpose of a writing assignment is to induct students into disciplinary conventions, the professor might find it useful to explain to students that the grading of such conventions would not necessarily extend to other disciplines. Such a reminder could be useful when students ask why Professor A in history graded the same paper differently from Professor B in philosophy.

Audience

The second pillar of writing assignments, audience, is inextricably related to the first pillar, purpose. In most writing situations beyond the classroom, authors want to know who will be reading a document so that the authors can write the document for that audience. Thus, one of the purposes in writing is to define the audience for a piece of writing. Fulfilling this purpose is extremely difficult because many, many documents have multiple audiences. Consider, for instance, a common document on college and university campuses: the student newspaper. Who is the primary audience for an article in the newspaper? The secondary audience? The tertiary audience?

Suppose that a journalism student writes on assignment an article for the newspaper. Suppose also that the journalism professor given oversight for the newspaper not only gives the student pointers during the writing process but also assigns a grade to the published article. Further suppose that the student editor for the newspaper has a tendency to make editorial changes in articles right before the articles go to press and without consulting with the journalism professor. Add to this layered writing process that includes multiple audiences an even more diverse audience for the school newspaper, including the journalism student's friends, acquaintances, sorority rivals, parents, spouse, and brother; professors from across campus who have taught, are teaching, and will teach the journalism student; staff members; administrators; and anyone else who has access to the newspaper.

Again, assume that an article with the journalism student's byline infuriated a prominent donor, who called the president of the university to express her displeasure. The president, in turn, unleashed the wrath of Achilles on the chair of the Journalism Department. Without tracing all the emotional, political, and personal consequences of one audience member's reading of the article, let's return to the beleaguered student journalist and ask again, Who is the audience for the piece she wrote?

Part of the answer to that question is that the importance of certain members of an audience may emerge after a piece has been launched. This insight, painfully learned at times, not only suggests that identifying and writing to multiple audiences can be extremely difficult but also that professors should impress upon students the need for analysis of the audience during the writing process. Ensuring that all audiences reading a document will be able to interpret the document the way the author intended for it to be interpreted is no easy task and probably impossible the more varied the audience. So analysis of the audience, which requires a deft touch, is a prime consideration when professors create writing assignments and students create documents in response to those assignments.

Problems associated with multiple audiences also apply to a supposedly simple document: a student's report card for one semester's work. Although not a piece of a student's writing, report cards nevertheless are interesting examples of how to interpret grades, an issue that concerns professors. What do those grades on a report card, in the form of single letters, represent? To the student who receives the grades, they may have one meaning. To the professor who gave a grade, the grade may have a different meaning. (And if the professor could see all the student's grades for a particular semester, the professor might change his or her interpretation of the grade he or she gave.) To the student's parents or spouse, the grades might be interpreted using criteria different from those either the student or the professor used. To university administrators, the grades are interpreted in yet another way, in part because administrators may not have information about the classroom context in which the grades were "earned." To legislators, the grades may be interpreted in political terms relating to credit hours and funding.

> *Those five letter grades A through E are a set of symbols. Each has no inherent meaning nor any reality in itself. Meanings that are attached to these symbols exist in the minds of faculty, the students, and all those who use them for various purposes.*
>
> *It should not be surprising, therefore, that a B in a course should have different meanings for the instructor, for the student, for the graduate school admission officer, and for the company recruiter.* (Weeks, 1978, p. 164)

Unlike the multiple audiences for grades, the sole audience for many classroom writing assignments, unfortunately, is the professor, generally a representative of a very narrow and select audience. Professors, by academic training and number, represent a small population. How many undergraduate students, once they receive the baccalaureate, will ever write for a professor again? Even if baccalaureate graduates in the world of work happen to write to a professor on occasion, most of the writing they do will probably be directed to other audiences. This issue of other audiences raises questions about the appropriateness of the professor as sole audience for a piece of classroom writing, and certainly raises issues about the relationship between ways that professors grade classroom writing and the ways other professionals evaluate writing in the world of work. If professionals evaluate writing using a set of criteria different from those professors use, the way writing is evaluated in the academy may not have a strong relationship to the way writing is evaluated outside the academy in the typical workplace (Hairston, 1981). Certainly, possible mismatches between grading in the academy and evaluation in nonacademic settings may be unimportant if the relationship between academic performance and nonacademic performance is negligible. That does not seem to be the case, however, especially in light of the stress employers place on grades as one evaluative point for job candidates and employers' continual grousing against academics for lack of adequate preparation students receive for writing in nonacademic settings (Andrews & Sigband, 1984; Sharplin, Sharplin, & Birdsong, 1986; Stine & Skarzenski, 1979). What can academics do to build bridges between academic and nonacademic writing tasks?

One place to start building such bridges is for academics to specify nonacademic audiences in writing assignments to prepare students for writing to audiences other than just the professor. For instance, a professor might include in a writing assignment the following specification for an audience: "This report will go to your boss, the director of the museum, and the regional manager of museum operations. The director is new to the job and has come from Wall Street, where she was an investment broker. She has an undergraduate degree in art history, but other than an internship in her senior year at college, she has never worked in a museum. She sees her role as revitalizing the relationship between the museum and the community, so she has asked you to write a proposal for creating a Board of Community Representatives. The regional manager, on the other hand, ..."

Specifying nonacademic audiences, however, is not sufficient. People other than the professor should read and comment on students' writing. In other words, specifying imagined audiences is only one possible answer to the problem of expanding the actual audience for students' writing. Indeed, one objection to imagined audiences for writing assignments is that students are put in a double bind. The professor specifies an audience or audiences for a writing assignment, but students' writing will be measured against the professor's concept of the specified audience (Ede & Lunsford, 1984). If the professor is the sole actual audience for the writing, the problem of limiting the audience has not been given enough attention. How, then, can the professor include actual representatives from various audiences?

The easiest way is to involve students' classroom peers in reading and commenting on students' writing (discussed later). Another way to expand representatives of the actual audience is to enlist professionals to evaluate and grade students' writing. The use of external evaluators (Sawyer, 1975) is one example of this approach. Even including more than one professor's reading of students' writing can provide both a wider sense of audience and an opportunity to create a dialogue about evaluation standards (Raymond, 1976).

Determining and Specifying What Is Essential and What Is Optional

The second general issue related to developing effective writing assignments is for the professor to separate the essential from the optional and to specify in writing the requirements of the assignment and the criteria that the professor will use to evaluate and grade students' writing. What is essential and what is optional when students fulfill a writing assignment? Must students follow APA style when writing a research paper? If so, such a requirement must be made explicit in writing at the outset of an assignment. Must students ensure that a paper is no more than 10 pages long? Again, such a requirement must be stated in writing when the writing assignment is introduced.

Why should the professor inscribe the writing assignment, including grading criteria, and distribute it to all students? First, the professor establishes a level playing field. Everyone in the class has access to the same information. Second, the professor can address questions about the writing assignment by referring to the document and encouraging students also to refer to the document to answer their questions. Of course, if the document is ambiguous in any way, the professor can explain that what seems to be ambiguous should be understood as freedom to make decisions (e.g., the paper is due anytime between the Monday before Thanksgiving break and the Monday after Thanksgiving break) or as an oversight that requires clarification (e.g., "I forgot to give a point value for organization, so here it is."). Third, later, when students are working through the process to complete the assignment, they have access to the document and can refer to it to answer questions that arise. Generally, after the professor introduces a writing assignment and goes over it in class, students cannot think of all the questions they will encounter because they have not gotten deeply enough into the assignment. After students have had more time to scrutinize the assignment, they generally have questions, and the written writing assignment can provide answers to questions that they might not have foreseen when they first reviewed the document. Fourth, the criteria the professor will use for evaluating and assigning a grade to students' writing are made explicit at the outset of the assignment. Students therefore are given the best opportunity for fulfilling the criteria because they have access to the criteria at the beginning of the assignment. Fifth, the process of committing a writing assignment to paper has a tendency to make professors more responsible for the assignment than if they had simply delivered the assignment orally. Writing has a way of making us responsible in ways that oral communication cannot. This responsibility is intensified when professors make public their written writing assignments, because professors demonstrate their ability to write cogently and precisely.

A word of caution, however, is necessary about the specificity of writing requirements for an assignment. When making explicit requirements, the professor should be able to justify them. Even if the students never ask why the professor is imposing a 10-page limit, the professor should ask himself or herself that question and provide a reasonable answer. I suspect two major reasons for page requirements. One, the professor wants to read only a certain number of pages for each student. This reason has some merit. For instance, a professor may know that it takes him or her about 4.5 minutes on average to read and mark one page of a student's writing for a particular assignment. With 35 students in the class and a limit of 5 pages per student, the professor will spend 787.5 minutes or 13.13 hours evaluating students' writing. Showing the math to students could help explain a page limit.

Conversely, professors may establish a page requirement to ensure that students write enough. Thus, a professor may insist that students write at least 8 pages, believing that students would not be able to address a topic adequately if they wrote 3- and 4-page papers. The problem with this approach, however, is that students may pad their papers to reach the requirement for number of pages, particularly if the professor does not help students use the writing process by stating due dates on the syllabus for draft one, two, three, and so on, and by providing instruction on how to write effectively for a particular assignment. Nevertheless, specific requirements should be outlined at the beginning of the assignment.

The problem with many specific requirements—number of pages, settings of margins, color of paper, use of passive voice, no use of contractions—is that they appear to be artificial to students, and, indeed, the professor may never have felt a need to justify the requirements, assuming that they were bona fide. Generally, specific requirements, such as 1-inch margins all around, except on the left side, which should be 1.5 inches, are derived from printing and binding requirements that may have no particular merit for students' papers. (In fact, requirements that sensible journal editors impose on scholars' manuscripts are designed to save work for the editor when the manuscript is typeset for publication.) Unless professors are inducting students into disciplinary conventions or expecting students to submit their papers for publication, specific format requirements may be quite arbitrary. If such requirements are arbitrary, what is the purpose of basing any part of the grade on them? Professors may want to consider justifying specific criteria instead of putting themselves in the position of failing to reflect critically on their writing assignment or falling prey to the accusation that bare obedience is the intention behind seemingly unjustified criteria.

Although much of this discussion has focused on format or mechanics, issues related to content also need to be made specific. For instance, a professor makes a major assumption when assigning a book review and does not give detailed instructions about what constitutes the appropriate content for a book review. In the main, students believe that a book review is a plot summary. The professor needs to explain to students that the book review should be organized according to disciplinary conventions for book reviews and should explain those conventions.

Because the bulk of this monograph concerns classroom writing that employs the writing process, the kind of writing for testing students, such as impromptu essay exams, is of less interest here. Professors, however, might want to consider the relationship between the purpose of a writing prompt for an in-class impromptu essay exam and the purpose of writing assignments based on the writing process. In an in-class writing prompt, a professor might ask students to compare and contrast *x* and *y*. The purpose of such an assignment is to find out what the students know about *x* and *y* and their relationship to each other. In a sense, the professor is asking students to demonstrate that they have acquired certain knowledge. Although students might come up with an interesting insight while writing to a prompt, the purpose of the in-class writing assignment should not be to ask students to explore a topic the same way they would explore a topic during the early stages of the writing process. Rather, the professor expects the students to produce a fairly cohesive piece of prose, not a discursive piece of writing that simply lists facts. (It is important to note that professors who evaluate in-class essays according to the same tenets they would use to evaluate a piece of writing a student creates by following the writing process do an injustice to students. An in-class essay is produced under conditions and time constraints widely different from a piece of writing that evolves through the writing process. To compare the two is to compare a rough draft in the early stages of the writing process with a finished piece of writing that a student has had ample opportunity to refine.) Therefore, professors should not assume that the directions to compare and contrast mean the same thing when used in the prompt for an in-class essay and in a writing assignment based on the writing process. Professors need to explicate in writing what they want students to do when comparing and contrasting *x* and *y* in a full-blown writing assignment.

Determining What Standards Will Be Used to Evaluate Students' Written Responses to the Assignment

Students should know at the outset of a writing assignment how their written work will be evaluated during the writing process and graded at the end of the process. This expectation is so reasonable that a professor's failure to comply with it is a bit puzzling. If students don't know how their written

SAINT PETER'S COLLEGE LIBRARY
JERSEY CITY, NEW JERSEY 0730[illegible]

work will be evaluated, how do they know where to put their effort in fulfilling the assignment? Indeed, how do they know what really counts in terms of evaluation? Certainly, quality in writing cannot be reduced to a matrix that does not include professional judgment, which cannot be specified completely. Nonetheless, as much as can be specified should be specified.

One difficulty of specifying criteria is that what is agreed upon by all is often given the most priority. For instance, a category such as grammar, mechanics, and spelling is particularly attractive for grading purposes, because a professor can point out a grammatical error and cite a writing handbook or some other authority to show that the error is not merely a matter of personal taste. The problem with traveling such a path of least resistance is that it obscures the need to analyze writing for other, more significant features, such as organization and content. If a student can fail a paper because he or she is a poor speller, then writing has been reduced to spelling ability, when, in fact, unless a student's spelling is horrendous, most of the time readers will be able to figure out what the student is saying. If spelling is the focal point of assessing writing, the professor would save a great deal of time and trouble by administering a spelling test instead of using writing as a platform for testing spelling ability. The problem with making spelling the focal point of a writing assignment is that the need for communicative effectiveness is minimized (Hirsch & Harrington, 1981), because spelling errors, in general, do not hinder students from communicating effectively. The real problem is social status. We tend to look down on people who misspell; when we catch a spelling error, we show our superior ability as language users. We may quickly forget that spelling English words is not a particularly easy task, in part, because English spelling rules allow for many exceptions. In addition, words that sound alike but are spelled differently can be confused (its and it's), the marking of possession is sometimes shown by an apostrophe (girls') and sometimes by a word's form (their), and so on.

The categorization of possible writing errors is a function of writing handbooks, which can be rather thick and contain lots of rules about *common* errors. The existence of such handbooks suggests that students have ample opportunity to make errors that are so numerous they can be grouped and listed year after year in each new handbook publishers produce. Professors, therefore, might consider how intractable common errors are and explain to students that when students are able to identify and correct common errors in their writing and in the writing of others, they set themselves apart from a good many people who continue to make common mistakes in their writing.

All this is not to say that grammar, spelling, and mechanics should not "count" in some way, but students should know that the reason such things count is not necessarily because of problems with communicative effectiveness; professors often figure out what a student is saying despite surface errors in the student's writing. The real problem is that such errors often irritate readers, who have become accustomed to high levels of correctness, and such irritation can easily be translated into a hypercriticism that feeds upon itself by looking for even more errors. The result is a hunt for errors that focuses on what is wrong with a student's writing, without much regard for what the student did correctly. When this hunt happens during the grading of classroom writing, grading is reduced to citing "obvious" errors.

The other extreme to a reductionist approach to stating grading criteria in the writing assignment is the abstract approach, which explains criteria in abstract terms: "The paper must have good content and be well organized." If that is the finest level of detail for grading criteria, the professor seems to be asking students to intuitively understand what *good content* and *well organized* mean without any further explanation. What exactly constitutes *good* content? How *well* is a paper organized when it is *well* organized? Figure 1 provides criteria professors can use to evaluate their writing assignments, and the next section of this monograph discusses various assessment procedures that a professor can use to specify criteria for an assignment. Examples of such procedures are included there. The point here is that a useful philosophy of assignment design takes into account the need to give a sufficient level of detail to explain evaluative criteria so that the professor can use those criteria to grade students' writing. In addition, students can use the criteria throughout the writing process to shape their writing.

A useful philosophy of assignment design gives a sufficient level of detail to explain evaluative criteria so that the professor can use those criteria to grade students' writing and students can use the criteria to shape their writing.

Critiquing Writing Assignments

Colleagues and students can play an important role in providing feedback about potential lapses in writing assign-

FIGURE 1

Criteria Professors Can Use to Evaluate Their Writing Assignments

1. Are the purposes of the writing assignment stated clearly? Where in the assignment have you told students:
   - How the assignment fits into the overall purposes of the course?
   - Why this particular writing assignment, rather than another assignment, best meets the purposes you believe are important?
2. Are the audiences for the students' writing specified? Where in the assignment have you told students:
   - Whom they should envision as readers of their writing?
   - What your role as the professor is, both as a member of the audience and the person who will determine whether the students have addressed the appropriate audiences?
   - What level of detail about the specified audiences students need to know to complete the assignment effectively?
3. Has the rhetorical context been stipulated? Where in the writing assignment have you told students about the social-political-economic contexts pertinent to the purpose and audiences for the assignment, such as:
   - Interpersonal relations of supposed or real persons in the assignment,
   - Rules that govern behavior,
   - Unstated but enforced policies,
   - External forces that mandate organizational changes,
   - Ethical ambiguities?
4. Have the requirements for the assignment been stated clearly? Where in the writing assignment have you stated requirements, such as:
   - Due dates for drafts,
   - The minimum number of references that must be cited,
   - Disciplinary conventions that must be followed,
   - Maximum number of pages you will accept for each student's response to the assignment?
5. Have options been addressed? Where in the writing assignment have you told students about the choices they have, such as:
   - Freedom to choose a topic,
   - Selection of a hard-to-read font,
   - Number of pages to produce in response to the assignment,
   - Choice of graphics,
   - Use of headings?

6. Have grading criteria been stated clearly? Where in the writing assignment have you told students:
- How each component of the assignment will be evaluated?
- What the point ranges are for letter grades?
- How grades will be calculated for collaborative writing projects?

7. Have model papers written in response to the writing assignment been provided? Where in the writing assignment have you directed students to examine model papers (e.g., at the reserve desk in the library or on a Web page for the class)?
8. Has the writing assignment been user tested?
- Have you asked a colleague or colleagues to review the writing assignment?
- Have you asked students in the class to read the writing assignment and explain it to you?

ments. As readers, they may be able to see gaps and inconsistencies in a writing that the writer is unable to spot because he or she is too close to the text, too engaged in creating a document to have the critical distance necessary to evaluate the document effectively. Thus, professors should consider showing drafts of their assignments to colleagues and asking for constructive criticism. Although such collegial feedback is undoubtedly often done informally, professors might even consider formalizing the process of collegial feedback by meeting regularly to critique each other's writing assignments and jointly grading one or two papers students produced to fulfill the assignment. When professors work collaboratively to discuss grading practices, they can help establish a dialogue about grading standards that can be extended to their entire department. When colleagues work with each other to ensure that writing assignments are carefully and cogently constructed, not slapped together a day before presenting the assignment to students, they can investigate the logical progression from writing assignment to graded paper.

Students also can provide insight into ways that a writing assignment might be improved before the students begin writing for the assignment, so professors might consider consulting with students about the intelligibility of a writing assignment. To do so, a professor could prepare a draft of an assignment, ask colleagues to review it, make any changes that seem appropriate, and give the assignment to his or her class for further review. Such a review serves two functions. First, students have an opportunity to read the assignment carefully during class and raise questions about how to interpret the assignment. Second, this intensive investigation of the assignment has the potential to raise questions that can be addressed in a revision of the assignment before the professor formally makes the assignment. The simplest way the professor can get feedback from students is for the professor to take the role of the uninformed participant and ask students to explain the assignment. Thus, the professor can say, "I wasn't in class today, so can you explain the writing assignment I heard about? Is it really true that Speck set a 25-page limit?" By asking students to explain the assignment in detail—and as an uninformed participant intentionally misinterpreting critical aspects of the assignment—the professor puts students in a position to focus on and articulate requirements of the assignment.

Conclusion

Of course, all that has been said about constructing writing assignments requires that professors plan ahead of time to integrate writing assignments with course objectives and determine what weight each assignment will have in relation to the entire course grade. Thus, writing assignments should be seen as a component of the entire course, and the professor should clearly understand course goals and be able to articulate those goals in writing, including inscribing the writing assignment. Without such an understanding, it could be extremely difficult for a professor to create effective writing assignments.

FAIRNESS AND PROFESSIONAL JUDGMENT

A variety of methods are available for classroom grading of students' writing, but which method should a professor use in grading students' written responses to any particular writing assignment? The answer to that question is not apparent, because conflicting perspectives about reliability, validity, fairness, and professional judgment both complicate the question and create a dichotomy. On the one hand, one group of professionals believe that the outcome of writing, a grade or score, should be justified using rigorous standards of psychometric or statistical analysis. This group of professionals are primarily interested in ensuring that the students' written products are graded according to canons of statistical measurement. On the other hand, another group of professionals question whether statistical measurements have the capability to determine the quality of a piece of writing. These professionals want writing evaluation to include both the process a student uses to write and the product the student creates by using that process. These professionals believe, rightly so, that the process and product are quite complex and depend upon each student's personal abilities, inclinations, and capability for growth at any particular developmental level, so teachers need to render professional judgments that cannot be fit into statistical methods. Some of these professionals believe that teachers' judgments need to be translated into grades; others believe that grades are inimical to the writing process and to learning (Bleich, 1997).

Professionals who at one end of the writing evaluation continuum advocate standardized tests of writing and on the other end advocate teachers' autonomy do not represent everyone on the continuum. Professionals on either end of the continuum need to become involved in a dialogue with each other about grading methods (White, 1995). Nevertheless, the two groups of professionals at either end of the continuum do represent pronounced and conflicting viewpoints about grading students' writing, so any discussion of grading methods needs to be introduced by a discussion of theoretical issues related to reliability, validity, fairness, and professional judgment.

Theoretical Issues Related to Reliability, Validity, Fairness, and Professional Judgment

If a person is a reliable employee, he or she is consistent, comes to work every day, and does the same quality of work day after day. The level of quality is not at issue because an employee can perform at a consistently low level of achievement and be reliable. An unreliable employee is one on whom you cannot depend, because the person may or may not come to work and may or may not get the job done. This understanding of employees' reliability is comparable to reliability in grading and awarding grades. If a professor is reliable in his or her method of grading students' writing, the professor will give the same quality of help to each student during the writing process. For instance, the professor will give consistent advice about revising to every student working on a particular writing assignment. When the professor assigns grades, the grade for student S will be justified on the same grounds as the grade for students R, P, and so on. The judgments the professor makes also will be reliable over time, so should the professor be asked after six months to regrade paper Z, the professor will be able to give paper Z the same grade within an acceptable range. (Paper Z received a C the first time and a C– six months later.) Reliability, however, is not limited to one professor's grading.

Reliability also refers to the evaluation habits among professors who are grading the same writing assignment. This interrater reliability is really quite important, because it serves as a point of checks and balances, helping to establish whether the grading process is fair. In addition, reliability is the basis for accountability, which is linked with generalizability. If, for instance, institution M is asked to accept transfer credit for students who attend institution O, then institution M should be very interested in the reliability of the grades institution O awards. Not only should institution M want to know whether any particular grade from institution O is reliable, but also whether the grades institution O awards have predictive reliability. That is, to what extent do the grades institution O awards predict the success students from institution O will have at institution M? Predictive reliability is what employers want when they look at a job applicant's grades. Do the As and Bs the job applicant was awarded as a chemistry major help the employer predict how successful the job applicant will be as a working chemist? Do the Cs and Ds the job applicant was awarded as an English major predict how successful the job applicant will be as an editor for a scientific publication?

Like reliability, validity also is concerned about fairness by answering the following question: Is what you're doing what you think you're doing? If, for instance, a person thinks that he or she is measuring a room to order carpet for that room, but the measurements are actually used to order wallpaper, then the person cannot be said to have reached valid results. The room measurements can be absolutely accurate, but they are not being used to measure what the person thought they were being used to measure. The same can be said for grading students' writing. A professor can be absolutely correct in saying that a student had three comma splices, four split infinitives, one fragment, two run-on sentences, a misplaced modifier, and two errors in subject-verb agreement, but what does the factual correctness of such an analysis tell anyone about the quality of a student's writing? If errors of the sort listed do say something about writing quality, what is it that they say?

Validity is still more complicated because it can be divided into internal and external validity. Internal validity refers to the isolation of the variable or variables a person is evaluating. For instance, a professor may want to know why student Jerome is consistently late for class on Thursdays. Is Jerome late because he has an evening class on Wednesday? Because he has a late appointment after the Wednesday class? Because Wednesday begins at 4:30 A.M. for Jerome when he has to help with his sister's paper route? Because Jerome doesn't know how to schedule his time well and waits until after the Wednesday class to do his assignments for the Thursday morning class? Because Jerome has a defective alarm clock? And on and on. As complicated as Jerome's case might be, isolating the variables for evaluating writing is a great deal more complex, so the question remains, Is the professor evaluating for construct *xyz?* If so, how does the professor know that what his or her evaluation yields is an assessment of *xyz* and not *xayz?* Has the professor controlled for all the other variables that could be the cause of the effect the professor is attempting to measure?

For example, professors often allow for wiggle room in their grading by including a category called "participation." This often nebulous category may be the basis for giving a student a low grade on a writing assignment, even when participation was listed in the syllabus as a separate category of evaluation. Thus, a professor, when assigning a grade to Jerome's essay, might remember, even subconsciously, that Jerome was sleeping in class on Thursday, after being late again, and give Jerome a B– instead of a B. The professor has just confounded the variables of writing performance with a variable of classroom performance that may or may not have anything to do with either Jerome's writing ability or writing performance (the two are not synonymous).

Maybe Jerome's performance on a writing assignment is not very good because the writing assignment is not clear and complete. If Jerome's writing performance is linked with the writing assignment—and it is—and the writing assignment is flawed, then when the professor measures Jerome's writing performance based on the assumption that the writing assignment is acceptable, Jerome is getting the blunt end of the evaluation stick. Jerome's grade is not valid.

The other type of validity is external validity. How generalizable is the grading process the professor used to evaluate and grade Jerome when it is applied to Jerome's classmates, students in different sections of the class taught by the same professor, students in different sections of the class taught by other professors, students in the same department who complete similar writing assignments, students throughout a campus who complete similar writing assignments, and students in a country and ultimately in the world who complete similar writing assignments? The question about validity becomes, How generalizable must a grading method be to be considered generalizable?

Generalizability, however, is even more complicated when writing assignments within a particular class are compared. If a professor uses one method of evaluating a writing assignment, such as a holistic scoring guide, and another method to evaluate another writing assignment, such as a checklist, can the professor demonstrate that the grades those methods produced are comparable? Is the A that student P received for his or her proposal the same as the A that he or she received for his or her letter to the editor? If the grades are not generalizable in comparison with each other, what is the relationship between not only the grades student P received but also the process the professor used to evaluate the students' writing process? If the professor is applying the same criteria and producing different results, then the criteria are flawed and not valid. If the professor is applying different criteria to different assignments, then what is the relationship among the grading processes used for the assignments?

The purpose in raising issues of fairness and the teacher's judgment in relationship to reliability and validity is not to provide definitive answers. First, we don't have definitive answers to many of the questions raised. Second, professionals don't even agree about the grounds for answers. Those on one end of the evaluative continuum are at odds with those on the other end of the continuum, and the position each group takes is based on differing theoretical premises. Third, writing is a complex activity that, as far as we know now, cannot be dissected into either process or product but must consist of both. How process and product relate to each other in terms of classroom evaluation is a matter of ongoing debate. Fourth, professors have little, if any, formal training in constructing writing instruments and assessing their grading performance in relation to standards of reliability and validity, so the practicality of insisting on the application of formal canons of statistical analysis to classroom writing performance is quite unrealistic, given our present system of preparing candidates for the professoriat. Nevertheless, professors should take it upon themselves to reflect upon issues related to reliability and validity in classroom grading, study the issues by reading some of the suggested sources in Figure 2, and adjust their classroom assessment practices to ensure greater fairness in terms of validity and reliability.

The practicality of insisting on the application of formal canons of statistical analysis to classroom writing performance is quite unrealistic, given our present system of preparing candidates for the professoriat.

Grading Methods

The grading methods discussed in this subsection can help a professor achieve greater validity and reliability, not necessarily in the strict statistical sense, but in the sense of making grading criteria visible at the beginning of a writing assignment and engaging students in the grading process. These methods will not be valid and reliable in the strict statistical sense inasmuch as they are developed for local classroom purposes. For instance, a rubric that is constructed jointly by professor and students reflects the concerns of a particular classroom and may have to be modified for another classroom. Moreover, it is not the case that because a method has an official label the method is reliable. A multiple choice examination is not valid and reliable because it fits in the category of multiple choice exams; rather, the exam must meet the requirements of reliability and validity. In the same way, a rubric is not valid and reliable just because it is a rubric. It might be a sterling example of what a rubric ought not to be. Any grading method, then, needs to be evaluated by the standards that govern the construction and use of that method. In addition, because the professor is the professional grading

FIGURE 2

Sources on Reliability and Validity in Grading Classroom Writing

Applebee, A. N., Langer, J. A., & Mullis, I. V. S. (1989). *Understanding direct writing assessment*. Princeton, NJ: Educational Testing Service.

Bauer, B. A. (1981). *A study of the reliabilities and the cost-efficiencies of three methods of assessment for writing ability*. ED 216 357.

Breland, H. M., Camp, R., Jones, R. J., Morris, M. M., & Rock, D. A. (1987). *Assessing writing skill*. New York: College Entrance Examination Board.

Breland, H., & Gaynor, J. L. (1979). A comparison of direct and indirect assessment of writing skill. *Journal of Educational Measurement, 16*(2), 119-128.

Calfee, R., & Perfumo, P. (Eds.). (1996). *Writing portfolios in the classroom: Policy and practice, promise and peril*. Mahwah, NJ: Erlbaum.

Cooper, C. (1975). Measuring growth in writing. *English Journal, 64*(3), 111-120.

Cooper, P. L. (1984). *The assessment of writing ability: A review of research*. Princeton, NJ: Educational Testing Service.

Davis, B. G., Scriven, M., & Thomas, S. (1987). *The evaluation of composition instruction* (2nd ed.). New York: Teachers College Press.

Fagan, W. T., Cooper, C., & Jensen, J. (1975). Measures: Writing. In *Measures for research and evaluation in the English language arts* (pp. 185-206). Urbana, IL: National Council of Teachers of English.

Faigley, L., Cherry, R. D., Jolliffee, D. A., & Skinner, A. M. (1985). *Assessing writers' knowledge and processes of composing*. Norwood, NJ: Ablex.

Gorman, T. P., Purves, A. C., & Degenhart, R. E. (Eds.). (1988). *The IEA study of written composition I: The international writing tasks and scoring scales*. Oxford, Eng.: Pergamon.

Greenberg, K. (1992). Validity and reliability: Issues in the direct assessment of writing. *WPA: Writing Program Administration, 16*(1-2), 7-22.

Hamp-Lyons, L. (1991). Basic concepts. In L. Hamp-Lyons (Ed.), *Assessing second language writing in academic contexts* (pp. 5-15). Norwood, NJ: Ablex.

Henning, G. (1991). Issues in evaluating and maintaining an ESL writing assessment program. In L. Hamp-Lyons (Ed.), *Assessing second language writing in academic contexts* (pp. 279-291). Norwood, NJ: Ablex.

Hewitt, G. (1995). *A portfolio primer: Teaching, collecting, and assessing student writing*. Portsmouth, NH: Heinemann.

Hughes, A. (1989). *Testing for language teachers*. New York: Cambridge University Press.

Huot, B. (1990). Reliability, validity, and holistic scoring: What we know and what we need to know. *College Composition and Communication, 41*(2), 201-213.

James, A. (1976). Does the amount written on assignments bias the grades awarded? *Teaching at a Distance, 7,* 49-54.

Legg, S. M. (1998). Reliability and validity. In W. Wolcott S. M. Legg (Eds.), *An overview of writing assessment: Theory, research, and practice* (pp. 124-142). Urbana, IL: National Council of Teachers of English.

Perkins, K. (1983). On the use of composition scoring techniques, objective measures, and objective tests to evaluate ESL writing ability. *TESOL Quarterly, 17,* 651-671.

Purves, A. C. (1992). Reflections on research and assessment in written composition. *Research in the Teaching of English, 26*(1), 108-122.

Quellmalz, E. S. (1986). Writing skills assessment. In R. A. Berk (Ed.), *Performance assessment: Methods and applications* (pp. 492-508). Baltimore: Johns Hopkins University Press.

Ranieri, P. W. (1988). Teachers, composition, competency, and the "beauty" of truth. *Rhetoric Review, 6*(2), 192-200.

Reckase, M. D. (1993, April). *Portfolio assessment: A theoretical prediction of measurement properties*. Paper presented at the annual meeting of the American Educational Research Association, Atlanta, GA. ED 358 138.

White, E. M. (1994). *Teaching and assessing writing* (2nd ed.). San Francisco: Jossey-Bass.

Williamson, M. (1994). The worship of efficiency: Untangling theoretical and practical considerations in writing assessment. *Assessing Writing, 1*(2), 147-173.

expert in the classroom, the interpretation of the effectiveness of any grading method depends on the professor's judgment regarding selection and design of classroom grading methods. In many ways, then, issues of classroom grading do revolve around professors' judgments, and those judgments begin with information about what the available means of grading are.

In general, most grading methods fall under the heading of rubrics. A rubric is a "scoring scale that clearly delineates criteria and corresponding values to evaluate students' performance" (Anderson & Speck, 1998, p. 2). Numerous example of rubrics are available, including rubrics for written assignments (Hobson, 1998), collaborative writing projects (K. Smith, 1998), writing for listservs (Morrison & Ross, 1998), inquiry projects (Busching, 1998), and portfolios (Scanlon & Ford, 1998). These various rubrics provide examples of how students' performance can be assessed, but the grading requirements of any particular classroom writing assignment can be articulated when the professor either adapts an existing rubric to a new or modified assignment or creates a rubric. (The next section of this monograph suggests a way to engage students in the development of a rubric.)

Primary trait scoring

One popular type of rubric is primary trait scoring, which is based on specified criteria. For instance, should a philosophy professor decide to evaluate students' essays on Plato's *Gorgias,* the professor would need to determine the criteria for such a paper. Let's say that the professor determines that students need to show that they understand Gorgias's argument, explain how Gorgias is representative of Sophist arguments, cite at least three of Socrates's objections to Gorgias's argument, and discuss two difficulties with Socrates's position. Each of these requirements requires elucidation, but for our present purposes the elucidation of one requirement will serve as a model for elucidating the other requirements. Let's take the first criterion—students need to show that they understand Gorgias's argument—and develop a primary trait scoring guide for it.

To develop the scoring guide for the first criterion, the professor will need to determine the components of Gorgias's argument, which are, according to the professor, that (a) the public speaker does not need to have knowledge of a particular subject to persuade an audience, (b) the truth about any topic is relative, and (c) the public speaker should find out what an audience wants and fit his argument to address those wants. So students will need to state those three components, but stating them is not sufficient, because the professor wants the students to provide examples from *Gorgias* for each component and wants the students to demonstrate good organizational and writing skills. The professor, after thinking about this requirement and preparing several drafts of a primary trait scoring guide, might come up with the one shown in Figure 3.

The philosophy professor has made a start and now needs to create a similar primary trait scale for each criterion in the writing assignment. Collectively, these scales constitute the

FIGURE 3

Primary Trait Scoring Guide for First Criterion of *Gorgias* Assignment

On the following scale, 4 is the highest level of achievement.

4 Identifies the three components of Gorgias's argument: (a) the public speaker does not need to have knowledge of a particular subject to persuade an audience, (b) the truth about any topic is relative, and (c) the public speaker should find out what an audience wants and fit his or her argument to address those wants. Provides significant examples from *Gorgias* for each component. Organizes his or her writing so that it is logical, one point leading necessarily to the next point. Includes transitions between each component and within each component. Few, if any, grammatical, mechanical, and spelling errors. Essentially good philosophical writing style.

3 Identifies the three components of Gorgias's argument. Provides adequate examples from *Gorgias* for each component. Writing is basically logical, but with a lapse in logic here and there. Lacks a few transitions between each component and within each component. Some grammatical, mechanical, and spelling errors. Fairly good philosophical writing style.

2 Identifies two of the three components of Gorgias's argument. Provides inadequate examples from *Gorgias* for each component. Writing has quite a few problems with logic so that the argument is hard to follow. Lacks many transitions between each component and within each component. Quite a few grammatical, mechanical, and spelling errors. Not very good philosophical writing style.

1 Identifies one of the three components of Gorgias's argument. Provides at least one example from *Gorgias* for the component identified. Writing is quite illogical, making it virtually impossible for a reader to follow the argument. Few if any transitions within the component. Many, many grammatical, mechanical, and spelling errors. Little, if any, resemblance to good philosophical writing style.

0 Even less merit than 1.

grading instrument students can consult as they go through the writing process to complete the writing assignment, and it is the instrument the professor will use to assign a grade to each student's writing.*

Holistic scoring

Whereas primary trait scoring focuses on specific criteria for various sections of a writing assignment, holistic scoring focuses on a global evaluation of the entire piece of writing. The primary trait scoring guide the philosophy professor produced for the first criterion of the *Gorgias* assignment is similar to an entire holistic scoring guide (Figure 4).

Clearly, the holistic scoring guide is not as finely tuned as the primary trait scoring guide. In fact, holistic scoring guides are commonly used to evaluate large-scale writing assignments, such as an impromptu entrance essay for placement purposes. Holistic scoring, when it is used properly to evaluate such placement essays, requires readers to be trained—calibrated—so that they agree on what constitutes a 4 or a 2 or a 0 for any essay. Unfortunately, some of the literature on classroom grading makes the leap from the calibration of readers to the use of a holistic scale by a single classroom professor. When a professor uses a holistic scale for the classroom grading process, the yield is a general impression of students' writing, not a valid and reliable holistic score. Nevertheless, a holistic scale, when it is given to students at the outset of an assignment, does provide them with some direction concerning the assignment and can give the professor some guidance in evaluating students' work and giving a grade to each one's writing.†

Assorted methods

Yet another wrinkle on a rubric is a checklist, which is just what it purports to be, a list of criteria the professor and student can "check off" during evaluation of the student's writ-

---

*For an example of how the primary trait scale's criteria can be converted to a grade, see Walvoord & Anderson, 1998, chap. 5, who also provide detailed instructions on how to develop a primary trait scale. Other useful sources include information about developing and administering primary trait scoring guides (Krupa, 1979; Meyers, 1988; Polanski, 1987; Walvoord, Anderson, Breihan, McCarthy, Robison, & Sherman, 1996; Wolcott & Legg, 1998, chap. 7).

†To learn more about holistic scoring of classroom writing, see Cameron, 1993; Lauer, 1989; Lotto & Smith, 1979; Najimy, 1981; Westcott & Gardner, 1984; Wolcott & Legg, 1998, chap. 7.

FIGURE 4

Sample Holistic Scoring Guide for *Gorgias* Assignment

On the following scale, 4 is the highest level of achievement.

4 *Superior* job of identifying the three components of Gorgias's argument, explaining how Gorgias is representative of Sophist arguments, citing at least three of Socrates's objections to Gorgias's argument, and discussing two difficulties with Socrates's position. Provides significant examples from *Gorgias* to back up the argument. Organizes writing so that it is logical, one point leading necessarily to the next point. Includes transitions between each component and within each component. Few, if any, grammatical, mechanical, and spelling errors. Essentially good philosophical writing style.

3 *Good* job of identifying the three components of Gorgias's argument, explaining how Gorgias is representative of Sophist arguments, citing at least three of Socrates's objections to Gorgias's argument, and discussing two difficulties with Socrates's position. Provides adequate examples from *Gorgias* to back up the argument. Organizes writing so that it is mostly logical. Generally includes transitions between each component and within each component. Some grammatical, mechanical, and spelling errors. Adequate philosophical writing style.

2 *Fair* job of identifying the three components of Gorgias's argument, explaining how Gorgias is representative of Sophist arguments, citing at least three of Socrates's objections to Gorgias's argument, and discussing two difficulties with Socrates's position. Provides too few examples from *Gorgias* to back up the argument. Has trouble organizing writing so that it is logical. Some transitions between each component and within each component are missing. Quite a few grammatical, mechanical, and spelling errors. Inadequate philosophical writing style.

1 *Inadequate* job of identifying the three components of Gorgias's argument, explaining how Gorgias is representative of Sophist arguments, citing at least three of Socrates's objections to Gorgias's argument, and discussing two difficulties with Socrates's position. Includes hardly any examples from *Gorgias* to back up the argument. Writing is quite illogical. Hardly any transitions between each component and within each component. Many grammatical, mechanical, and spelling errors. Lacks any philosophical writing style.

0 Even less merit than 1.

ing (Boss, 1988, 1989; Bryant, 1975; Hudgins, 1987; Tebeaux, 1980; Warren, 1976; Weaver, 1986).

A grading contract, while not a checklist, may or may not be in the form of a rubric. For instance, a contract may specify that so many "adequate" papers equals a C for the course (Dorazio, 1984) or be based on qualitative categories—publishable, revisable, rewrite, for example—with four publishable and two revisable essays equaling an A for the course (Beale & King, 1981) or be deemed "acceptable" or "unacceptable," with two acceptable papers equaling a D for the course (Knapp, 1976).* Figure 5 provides an example of a grading contract.

FIGURE 5

Sample Grading Contract

Grading Contract for Anthropology 2301

I, ________________, choose the following grade option for Anthropology 2301:*

☐ **Grade of A**

- Write 4 of the 4 position papers at the excellent level as specified in the syllabus.
- Write at least a 3-page double-entry journal for each reading assignment in the text authored by Sigsbee.
- Participate in 3 formal in-class debates at the more-than-adequate level as specified in the syllabus.
- Receive a Pass-4 on the midterm essay examination.
- Accrue at least 115 points for the weekly quizzes.
- Receive a Pass-4 on the final essay exam.
- Receive an Excellent for the portfolio project.
- Accrue no more than 2 absences and 2 tardies.

☐ **Grade of B**

- Write 3 of the 4 position papers at the excellent level as specified in the syllabus.
- Write at least a 2-page double-entry journal for each reading assignment in the text authored by Sigsbee.
- Participate in 2 formal in-class debates at the more-than-adequate level as specified in the syllabus.
- Receive a Pass-3 on the midterm essay examination.
- Accrue at least 105 points for the weekly quizzes.
- Receive a Pass-3 on the final essay exam.

*Other variations on these patterns are reported in the literature; see, e.g., Cripe, 1980; Delworth, 1973; Dickey, 1978; Friedman, 1974; Mandel, 1975; Proffitt, 1977; Radican, 1997; Wilson, 1979.

- Receive a Good for the portfolio project.
- Accrue no more than 3 absences and 3 tardies.

☐ **Grade of C**

- Write 2 of the 4 position papers at the excellent level as specified in the syllabus.
- Write at least a 1-page double-entry journal for each reading assignment in the text authored by Sigsbee.
- Participate in 1 formal in-class debate at the more-than-adequate level as specified in the syllabus.
- Receive a Pass-2 on the midterm essay examination.
- Accrue at least 95 points for the weekly quizzes.
- Receive a Pass-2 on the final essay exam.
- Receive a Fair for the portfolio project.
- Accrue no more than 3 absences and 3 tardies.

☐ **Grade of D**

- Write 1 of the 4 position papers at the excellent level as specified in the syllabus.
- Write at least a 1-page double-entry journal for each reading assignment in the text authored by Sigsbee.
- Participate in 1 formal in-class debate at the more-than-adequate level as specified in the syllabus.
- Receive a Pass-1 on the midterm essay examination.
- Accrue at least 85 points for the weekly quizzes.
- Receive a Pass-1 on the final essay exam.
- Receive a Poor for the portfolio project.
- Accrue no more than 4 absences and 4 tardies.

☐ **Grade of F**

- Write 0 of the 4 position papers at the excellent level as specified in the syllabus.
- Write at least a 1-page double-entry journal for each reading assignment in the text authored by Sigsbee.
- Participate in 0 formal in-class debates at the more-than-adequate level as specified in the syllabus.
- Receive a No Pass on the midterm essay examination.
- Accrue at least 75 points for the weekly quizzes.
- Receive a No Pass on the final essay exam.
- Receive an Unacceptable for the portfolio project.
- Accrue no more than 4 absences and 4 tardies.

____ (signed)

*This contract can be renegotiated after the fourth week of class. After the fourth week, the contract is nonnegotiable.

Checkmark grading (see, e.g., Buchholz, 1979; Freeman & Hatch, 1975; Haswell, 1983; Throop & Jameson, 1976) is designed to help students correct errors. Thus, the professor puts a checkmark in the margin of a student's paper indicating that an error is present in the line of text opposite the checkmark. The student must find the error and correct it before returning the paper to the professor for a grade. One problem with this method is that a student may not be able to identify errors. In addition, the method focuses on surface errors, which are only one facet of writing, a facet generally reserved for later stages in the writing process devoted to editing.

Although pass/no-pass grading (Collison, 1974; Dreyer, 1977; Houston, 1983; McDonald, 1973) appears to be based on a concern that grades be minimized, unless the registrar accepts pass/no-pass as legitimate grades, the professor must make more finely tuned decisions about grades at the end of the term. In addition, pass/no-pass grading can focus on substantive issues, such as organization and content, but a pass/no pass approach does not guarantee such a focus.

In an effort to distinguish between the professor's role as a helper and his or her role as a judge, professors have developed ways of separating grading from the grade.

In an effort to distinguish between the professor's role as a helper and his or her role as a judge, professors have developed ways of separating grading from the grade. For instance, in exchange grading (see, e.g., Raymond, 1976; Tritt, 1983), Professor A grades the papers of Professor B's students while Professor B grades the papers of Professor A's students. This exchange allows Professor A to focus on his or her role as a helper during the writing process and puts the job of giving a grade for students' writing in Professor B's lap. If a student contests the grade Professor B gives, Professor A can ask Professor C to grade the paper without reference to Professor B's grade. The student will receive the higher of the grades given by Professor B and Professor C. Professor C's role in the entire process is vital because it ensures that students can have a second opinion and will not be penalized for asking for one.

A slightly different take on exchange grading is external evaluators (Sawyer, 1975, 1976). The professor calls upon graders external to the class—for example, professionals working in a particular field, such as engineering—and asks them to grade students' work. External evaluators are particularly useful for courses in professional areas, such as engineering, social work, and health sciences, because students are being graded by people who represent their future employers and supervisors.

The virtue of these methods lies in their ability to promote the writing process, provide students with clear evaluative standards at the outset of an assignment, and allow for revision based on preliminary evaluations before a grade is administered. The methods discussed so far have the potential to meet those three criteria in varying degrees, but the last method of grading discussed here, portfolios, is considered by many to be the premier way to meet all three criteria.

Portfolios

A portfolio is a collection of a student's written work and can include not only finished drafts, but also examples of the various drafts a student wrote to get to the finished draft. Portfolios also can include examples of self-evaluations, peer reviews, grading criteria, and the student's own reflections on the entire process for a particular piece of writing and/or the entire process for creating the portfolio, including all the processes the student used to write the pieces in the portfolio. Portfolios have enormous potential to support the entire writing process, including the essential role of revision in that process. Indeed, advocates of using portfolios to grade classroom writing sing the praises of portfolios (see, e.g., Agnew, 1995; Belanoff, 1991, 1996; Gallehr, 1993; Gibson, 1992; Hewitt, 1995; Leder, 1991; Metzger & Bryant, 1993; Stern, 1991). What are the reasons for such praise?

First, portfolios, when properly used, are a logical culmination of the writing process. Students not only have the opportunity to take individual pieces of writing through the writing process, but they also have the opportunity to revise "final" drafts of various assignments for one last review during evaluation of the portfolio. Because revision is the heart of the writing process, portfolios allow maximum opportunities for revision, and when professors evaluate a student's portfolio, they can reward the student for taking time either to polish or significantly improve particular pieces. To encourage such polishing and improvement, professors can allot time toward the end of the term for students to revisit and revise pieces they had the opportunity to take through the writing process. Thus, portfolios extend the writing process as much as possible, given the limitations of a one-quarter or one-semester class.

Second, portfolios allow students the opportunity to reflect upon their work. For instance, a professor can ask students to assemble a portfolio of their work during the quarter or semester and evaluate that work by writing rationales for the pieces in the portfolio. Let's say that a professor of business management wanted each student in the class to create a growth portfolio, one that showed how much each student had grown in his or her understanding of business management throughout the course. Further, let's suppose that the professor had assigned a number of writing assignments that could be included in the portfolio. The professor could ask students to select no more than five writing assignments, to write a rationale for each assignment explaining why the writing the student did to fulfill that particular assignment demonstrated the student's growth in understanding business management, and to write a preface and conclusion for the portfolio. Such a portfolio assignment provides students with the opportunity to reflect upon and to write about their learning. Students not only have to make decisions about what to include in their portfolios, but they also have to write justifications for their choices. Self-evaluation of this sort certainly can be useful in promoting critical thinking and evaluation skills.

Third, portfolios, when aligned with the writing process, promote the essential collaborative nature of writing by encouraging students to confer with each other and the professor about their writing. For instance, when students talk with each other about their writing, they can gain insights about how to revise their work, how to explain more carefully what they intended (or didn't intend) to say. Talking about writing also can promote a community of writers who learn and practice skills in reading writing from the perspective of a coach, not a judge. In short, portfolios offer opportunities for professors to take advantage of the writing process to help students become better writers.

Fourth, portfolios provide a comprehensive view of the writing students do during a course, and professors can therefore evaluate a student's writing performance in toto, not merely piecemeal. Indeed, if the portfolio includes drafts of particular pieces of writing, the professor can analyze the drafts to determine whether students have put enough effort into revising their writing, whether the quality of students' writing has improved throughout the class, and whether students' total writing output is sufficient evidence for a particular grade. Thus, the final grade for students' writing (or at least a major part of the course grade, if individual pieces have been graded already) is based on the student's total output. Portfolios, then, really can support the integration of the writing and grading processes.

Evaluating portfolios is problematic, however. For instance, evaluating portfolios can conflict with other grading systems (Christian, 1993). What is the relationship between the individual grades students received on particular writing assignments and the grade they receive for their portfolio? Or what is the relationship between a grade based on a checklist rating for one writing assignment, a primary trait score for another writing assignment, and a holistic rating for the portfolio? In addition, portfolios may be difficult to evaluate when a student's writing involves multiple genres (Hamp-Lyons & Condon, 1993). Should a letter to the editor of the local newspaper be given the same weight as a memo to a fictional audience? What is the grading relationship between an argumentative essay and a research paper, which are both included in the portfolio? Portfolios also raise questions about validity, reliability, and bias (e.g., Myers, 1996; Nystrand, Cohen, & Dowling, 1993; Reckase, 1993). For instance, untrained portfolio evaluators may not rate portfolios at acceptable levels of reliability. And it may be the case that the order of a student's written products (either by quality or genre) can bias evaluators' ratings.

In addition, is it reasonable to expect that professors will have the time necessary at the end of a term to evaluate each student's portfolio thoroughly? Will professors examine drafts of students' papers to determine whether students have revised them sufficiently? Indeed, do professors have a way of measuring revisions students make to determine whether a particular student's revisions are sufficient? Isn't the quality of the final written product the acid test of the quality of a particular piece of writing? And what about the hope that students will take time toward the end of a term—when they are experiencing pressure from other courses in which final papers are due—to revise their work? Is such a hope realistic? These questions should give professors pause when they consider using portfolios in their classes, but the questions should not stop professors from experimenting with portfolios.

In assigning portfolios to my students, I have discovered that students find the experience of putting together a portfolio quite rewarding, in part because they have the opportunity to review all the work they have done and to construct a document that has meaning for them. In grading portfolios, professors might want to focus on the quality of final drafts and the quality of the justifications students write for individual selections they include in their portfolios. As in all grading, professors need to make their grading criteria explicit at the beginning of the portfolio assignment, but, in addition, they need to ensure that the method for grading the portfolio does not penalize students who have adhered to the grading criteria for other classroom assignments. Grading portfolios needs to be integrated with the grading scheme for the rest of the class assignments.

Conclusion

What should be evident at this point is that evaluating writing takes a great deal of time. Portfolios are one of the most time consuming methods for professors and for students. Like the other methods discussed in this section, however, portfolios provide the professor with options for evaluating students' writing, options that fit with the writing and grading processes. Which option a professor chooses for any particular assignment will depend on the course's goals for writing, time the professor is willing to spend in evaluating writing (including, of course, peer evaluation during and outside of class), the amount of instruction the professor is willing to provide students about the writing and grading processes, and the amount of time the professor is willing to spend on ongoing faculty development by reading literature about grading. The critical person in classroom grading is the professor. Professors who are willing to learn more about grading will find a wealth of sources (including those cited in this monograph) to guide them in their journey as classroom promoters of writing.

INCLUDING STUDENTS IN THE ASSESSMENT OF WRITING

The impulse *not* to include students in the grading process is strong in the academy, so before discussing ways professors *can* include students in the grading process, it is necessary to address the predisposition that objects to students' involvement in grading. On the face of it, the predisposition against students' involvement is hard to justify, as students are the ones who create text in response to a writing assignment; students are not passive as text producers and are already actively engaged in the writing process. As text producers, aren't students already, even necessarily, participants in the grading process? Yet when the suggestion is advanced that students should be formally engaged in actively evaluating their writing and their peers' writing, two appeals are made to academic integrity. The first appeal is to professorial responsibility and authority to administer the grading process, including grades. The second is to providing safeguards to control cheating, specifically plagiarism. Both appeals, while grounded in a legitimate concern for academic integrity, take a narrow view of grading that can be widened considerably by acknowledging the legitimacy of intertwining the writing and grading processes. Therefore, let's investigate each appeal in relation to those intertwined processes.

Professorial Authorities

The appeal to professional authority is problematic because it does not adequately distinguish among professorial authorities: official authority, subject matter authority, and teaching authority (Speck, 1998b, pp. 21-25). These authorities can overlap, but it is not the case that because a teacher is an expert in his or her field (subject matter authority) he or she possesses the skills needed to be a good teacher (teaching authority). Certainly, professors have been entrusted with the authority to make judgments in the form of grades about students' performance (official authority), but that does not mean that professors have the requisite knowledge or skills to make such judgments effectively. If academic training in a content area were sufficient to ensure that professors were excellent teachers, why are some professors with excellent training in their area of specialty less than excellent teachers?

The suggestion that official authority is sufficient to guarantee effective grading of students' writing is based on an appeal to official authority that, to have integrity, must be integrated with teaching and subject matter authority. Ideally, official authority is grounded in subject matter authority and teaching authority; in higher education, however, such an ideal is often not supported by the reality of how people are trained for the professoriat or by professors' degree of involvement in faculty development.

Yet it remains the case that professors have formal authority to award grades, even when they lack subject matter and teaching authority. How then can professors responsibly exercise formal authority in relation to subject matter and teaching authority? Part of the answer to that query is that professors *should* integrate all three authorities, and it is questionable whether the three can be integrated successfully when the focus is on formal authority. Here theory about the writing process helps because we learn that students need to have authority as writers to write effectively (Brannon & Knoblauch, 1982). Thus, students—or any writer for that matter—need to have not only the responsibility for making choices about their writing but also the authority to make those choices. In other words, writers need to have both the freedom and skill to make effective writing choices, implying that the professor cannot exercise formal authority effectively without using subject matter and teaching authority to enable students to emulate the authorities the professor possesses. Professors best use their integrated authorities by enabling students to exercise authority to evaluate, to learn, and to help others grow as writers. Although this discussion of authorities inevitably leads to an exploration of learning theories, a topic beyond the purview of this monograph, the essential point here is that students learn to write by being given the freedom to investigate their writing process and the tools necessary to develop their writing skills. Professors in all disciplines have an obligation to help students write effectively for those disciplines by providing a classroom environment in which students gain skill in writing and are given the opportunity to make choices about their writing. Without skills in writing, students may not even be aware of choices. Without freedom, they believe that they must follow a prescribed format—in virtually every detail—to be successful writers.

The educational establishment has so inculcated in students the notion that certain writing skills are essential as to cause them to believe categorically that the purpose of writing is to avoid errors. In addition, the educational establishment has so inculcated in students the notion that prescribed format is paramount so as to cause them to ask, virtually immediately after a writing assignment has been introduced, "How long should our papers be?" If the educational establishment were more concerned with promoting skill *and* choice, as they can be promoted through the writing process to help students gain authority and responsibility as writers, then the first request students would make after the introduction of a writing assignment might very well be, "Tell us more about what constitutes a quality paper in terms of depth of analysis and presentation of that analysis for our intended audience." Professors can be instrumental in encouraging students to refocus their attention on quality instead of focusing on compliance with formal authority devoid of critical analysis of its value and wisdom.

To refocus students' attention on the intertwined writing and grading processes, the professor can use the writing process to help students understand more about quality issues related to analysis and presentation of the analysis. Quality, however, relies upon a student's skill and freedom to make choices, choices that may not work. Learning, after all, is a process that includes fumbles and failures, and part of the professor's goal in helping students learn to write is to allow students the freedom to fail. If students are not free to fail, they are not free to succeed and produce quality work. This observation is particularly true with writing because writing is an important way of thinking and learning. Writing is not transcribing what is already completely formed in the mind; writing is discovering what the writer has to say and needs to learn about a topic for the purpose of expressing himself or herself in relationship to others. In addition, writing is not only the means to record the conversation about ideas that has been in progress for thousands of years and thus can be traced by the various print sources extending back to the beginning of writing, but also an important means of participating in that conversation.

Cheating

The second appeal to academic integrity is concerned with cheating, specifically plagiarism in writing instruction. While plagiarism, when done consciously with the intent to deceive, is particularly egregious, the central concern with plagiarism is often *individual* performance, without sufficient consideration of the essential collaborative nature of writing

(Howard, 1995). If the major purpose of writing instruction is to determine students' originality as writers—what *they* have to say about a topic—then plagiarism is of paramount importance. Such a purpose is so lofty, however, that it essentially negates the purposes for which writing is generally taught and used in the academy and elsewhere. For instance, scientific papers in the IMRAD format are generally not displays of written originality. They are, in fact, quite purposefully unoriginal because the focus is on the use of scientific principles to discover a solution to a scientific inquiry, such as determining how a particular virus works so that it can be disarmed. And most discoveries are incremental, building on one another to produce a scientific insight worthy of a major advance in a particular discipline. Even the language used to announce the discovery may not be an example of brilliant scientific prose style.

The seeming lack of concern about originality extends to various other documents, such as business letters, annual reports, computer manuals, popular magazines, newspapers, and so on. These documents are quite unoriginal in that they are fairly predictable both in form and content. Readers expect certain features from a popular magazine, and publishers standardize those features so that readers will anticipate them when the next issue of the document—a magazine or a computer manual, for example—arrives. The same is true of business letters. Recipients expect certain features in a business letter, including the way arguments are delivered. Those of us who receive marketing letters unannounced in our mailbox have a good idea of what the "pitch" will entail once we begin reading the letter. In other words, documents can be categorized by genre, which means that documents in a particular genre have similar features. Part of the idea behind teaching students to write a laboratory report, for instance, is to inform them about the features of that particular genre.

Although a discussion of genre might seem to stray from the appeal to academic integrity and plagiarism in writing, it is important to recognize that when professors teach students to comply with the features of a particular genre, the professors are passing on knowledge they themselves received. They probably don't preface their comments about laboratory reports, scientific papers, or personal essays with academic references to the origin of those genres, but rather assume the acceptance of the genres and treat them as matter of fact. That is, professors assume that collaboration is a fact of academic life by drawing willingly, perhaps unselfconsciously, from the well of collective knowledge when they teach.

This same matter of factness about collaboration is characteristic of writing. Writers appeal to a common body of knowledge without feeling a great deal of obligation to cite sources for every such appeal. They naturally borrow from other writers. This fact is no less true of academic authors and is particularly obvious when their writings are read from the perspective of graduate students. In a class I team teach on research methods, the graduate students are required to write a literature review. Frequently, after reading literature on a particular topic, a graduate student asks penetrating questions about academic documentation, noting that scholars seem to take a great deal for granted when they make arguments. They do. They assume that their readers have been engaged in reading the same literature the writers have been reading. They allude to an author's argument in passing without providing a citation for the allusion. They may make a pun at the expense of a particular theory, assuming that the readers are aware of the theory and will delight in the pun. They use shorthand references to particular sources, perhaps using nomenclature for a theory that only insiders know. In other words, academic authors not only make assumptions about their audiences' background but also borrow freely from others when making arguments; moreover, they do not feel obligated to cite every source they use. (Because most scholarly works are submitted to peers for review and to editorial scrutiny—both substantive and copyediting scrutiny—we can reasonably assume that the existence of free borrowing is endorsed by the academic disciplines in which such borrowing is found.) Perhaps it is not possible to write with originality without either explicitly or implicitly alluding to a host of people who have laid the foundation for the seemingly *original* thought a scholar articulates.

All of which is to say that writing is essentially a collaborative activity and that the grading of writing should include a healthy dose of awareness of conventions that support writing efforts. That these conventions can be manipulated for good effect is not at issue. Genres appear, disappear, and reappear revitalized though emendation. What is at issue is the belief that writing is an individual activity that should be evaluated in terms of individual effort. Frankly, most classroom writing is not evaluated on the basis of originality but on the basis of conformity to conventions. Yet those who want to protect academic integrity by insisting on individual writing efforts do not seem to recognize that conformance to conventions is a collaborative effort that requires a set of conventions a group of people have agreed on. Even the rhetoric—the way arguments are framed and delivered—students are taught in various disciplines is generally a matter of convention. Yet students are thought to be cheating when they collaborate *with each other* to help each other figure out how to become effective writers. In other words, when novices help novices, they may be violating academic integrity, but when novices consult with experts, they are not violating academic integrity. This argument seems odd, unless a person is saying that when novices consult with each other, they intend to violate academic integrity, but then such an argument would have to include interaction between novice and expert. Or perhaps a person would say that novices, because of their status as uninformed participants, have a greater tendency to violate academic integrity. Although it seems to be the case, the remedy is effective teaching that engages novices in the grading process, not more restrictions that continue to enforce a novice's uninformed status.

Students are thought to be cheating when they collaborate* with each other *to help each other figure out how to become effective writers.

If an important role the professor plays is to extend teaching and grading authority to students, then the professor might consider the collaborative nature of writing. What exactly is the relationship between individual effort in writing and the grading of writing? Is it possible or desirable for professors to enforce individual effort at the expense of not including students in the grading process by ensuring that they do not give feedback to their peers? Should students be forbidden from going to the writing center on campus and receiving professional assistance? Should professors refuse to give students pointers on how to improve their writing before the professors assign grades? Some of these questions border on the ludicrous, but they serve to tighten the focus on individual effort in writing as a function of academic integrity. Such a focus is too simplistic and tends to undercut the salutary influence of the process approach to writing and to grading writing. Certainly, collaborative writing is a well documented practice, both inside and outside the classroom (Speck, Johnson, Dice, & Heaton, 1999), so ample evidence exists to question the assertion that students should do original work when they write, meaning *individual* work.

Preparing Students to Make Informed Decisions About the Quality of Writing

One of the most powerful arguments in favor of including students in the grading process is that one purpose of teaching students how to write is to prepare them to write in various contexts throughout their lives. Professors throughout a campus are teaching students not only disciplinary conventions and writing skills but also how to analyze disciplinary arguments so as to determine what counts as evidence and to learn how to use successfully a discipline's rhetoric in framing arguments. The ability to analyze arguments and to create effective arguments based on such analysis can be marshaled on sundry occasions to write a variety of documents. Thus, students gain expertise that can aid them throughout their lives by analyzing not only the discourse of their disciplines but also the discourse of other disciplines.

Pragmatically, when students learn how to evaluate writing, they are learning skills for a task many of them will be asked to do as part of their jobs in nonacademic settings. Today's college graduate is tomorrow's assistant manager, who will have to be able to write narratives for employee evaluations, communications with a company, communications to constituents outside the company, and applications for other jobs within the company or elsewhere. Writing is a fact of nonacademic life for most college graduates.

When students learn how to evaluate writing, they are learning skills for a task many of them will be asked to do as part of their jobs in non-academic settings.

Ethical questions about how professors should prepare students to write in nonacademic settings naturally arise because collaborative writing raises issues about responsibility and because professors may be concerned about reducing writing to a pragmatic task designed for promoting the military-industrial complex. Although some professors argue that the academy is not a training ground for the personnel departments of business, industry, and government, the reality is that the academy is a part of the economic structures that support the social order. This fact does not mean that professors should not address sticky ethical issues related to writing because college graduates might not succeed in nonacademic settings if their consciences are too easily pricked. Rather, professors should address ethical issues concerning the role of writing in policy decisions and the evaluation of writing in relation to belief systems. Some of these issues can be addressed during the grading of writing when students help each other consider ethical concerns related to purpose and audience (Speck & Porter, 1990).

The next section of this monograph addresses two further assumptions that mitigate against professors' actively involving students in the grading process. Those assumptions are that students automatically learn from professors' responses to their written work and that a final grade plus the teacher's comments provide a learning experience for students. These assumptions are based on the premises that professors know how to give comments that will help the students learn, that the relationship between writing assignments is such that what a student learned on one assignment is transferable to another assignment, and that students know how to interpret professors' comments and translate them into future success in writing. Each of these premises is highly questionable.

To summarize, the professor has a significant opportunity to use his or her formal, subject matter, and teaching authorities to students' advantage by recognizing that writing is deeply indebted to the collaborative efforts reaching back to the inception of writing communication. Academic integrity need not be at risk when professors engage students in the grading process, because students' grading of writing—their own and others'—is naturally entwined with the writing process. Not to include students in the grading process mitigates against a pedagogical purpose of writing, which is to train students how to evaluate the quality of writing and how to use their skills as writers to improve their own and others' writing. The question now is, How can professors include students in the grading process?

Ways to Include Students in the Grading Process

The task of including students in the grading process takes time to plan and to implement, so a professor who decides to involve students in the grading process may want to develop a step-by-step plan that can be implemented over several semesters. To attempt in one semester to implement every evaluative technique that follows would be a Herculean task and would be quite impractical for professors who need class time for reasons other than helping students use and improve their writing. Nevertheless, the following techniques provide professors with a cabinet of tools that can help them teach students how to become more thoughtful and proficient assessors of writing.

Ask students to help develop a grading instrument
Professors who have not used rubrics may want to create a rubric for one writing assignment (see Figure 6). Instead of creating a rubric and giving it to the class for review, a professor might want to engage the class in creating a draft rubric. This would include explaining to the students what a rubric is, perhaps showing a model of a rubric, and taking time in class to discuss the relationship between the rubric and the writing assignment. For instance, if a major purpose of a writing assignment is to induct students into disciplinary conventions of a particular written form, the professor needs to help students echo those conventions in the rubric. One of the goals, then, is to help students identify the criteria that should be embedded in a writing assignment and specify values for each criterion or set of criteria. It follows that the development of a rubric need not be based on a totally democratic process, such as taking votes, but might be more in line with the political process of advice and consent.

Involving students in the development of a rubric is time consuming because students may be new to the level of evaluative engagement in which the professor is asking them to participate. From my experience in engaging students in evaluation of rubrics, one of the most time consuming factors, particularly for undergraduates, is getting students past the belief that a rubric should give significant weight to grammar, mechanics, and spelling. These features of language seem to be the foci of much secondary school training in writing, so students believe that attention to surface errors in grammar (subject-verb agreement), mechanics (the uses of commas), and spelling should play a significant part in evaluating writing. When students create rubrics with surface errors as a cornerstone of the grading process, they often receive low grades on their writing assignments because surface errors represent common errors that many students have not mastered. Moving the students toward discussion of higher level issues, such as organization, sentence structure, diction, and so forth, can be facilitated when the writing assignment stresses the importance of higher level issues.

The professor can assign a student or group of students to construct a rubric based on initial class discussions about the

FIGURE 6

Sample Rubric for a Writing Assignment

Rubric for Writing Assignment #1

Organization

- Thesis statement is clearly stated in the introduction.
- Rationale for thesis is developed logically throughout the paper.
- Conclusion is drawn logically from the rationale.
- Transitions are effective throughout the paper.

Content

- Paper focuses on topic and does not bring in subsidiary issues.
- Reasoning is clear, using valid logic.
- Key points are supported by appropriate evidence.
- Creative approach is used to discuss topic.

Usage

- Subjects and verbs agree throughout.
- No incorrect verb tenses are used.
- No run-on sentences, sentence fragments, or comma splices are used.
- No dangling modifiers are used.

Mechanics

- Punctuation is correct.
- Capitalization is correct.
- Spelling is correct.

Numerical Weight/Value

	Weight/Value	**Total Points**
Organization	3	15
Content	4	20
Usage	2	10
Mechanics	1	5
Total		50

writing assignment or can create a rubric himself or herself. If the professor selects a group of students to develop a rubric, the group should prepare a draft copy for the class to review, revise the draft based on input from the class and the professor, give the class the revised rubric for another review, and so on until the class agrees that the rubric is acceptable. Students can be responsible for providing their peers with copies of the completed rubric. If the professor develops a rubric, a draft of the rubric should be given to students so that they can give input for the creation of the final rubric.

Once a professor has worked with students to create a rubric for a writing assignment, that rubric need not be re-created for every other class that will be given the same assignment. The rubric a former class used can be presented as a draft to later classes, however, so that students in those classes can suggest ways to improve the rubric. Indeed, the professor might have revised the writing assignment for the rubric and may want to enlist students' help in comparing the old rubric with the revised writing assignment.

Notice that the development of the rubric assumes the existence of a writing assignment. If, as was stated earlier, the writing assignment should go through a similar process of advice and consent that involves students, and if the assignment and rubric should be available at the beginning of an assignment, the professor must allow time for the class's input into the writing assignment and attendant rubric. The rubric, however, need not be created at the outset of an assignment. Perhaps students need time to prepare a first draft based on the writing assignment before they are able to have insight into what criteria they should be evaluated on. Sometimes a writing assignment can appear to be one thing in students' eyes in the convivial classroom atmosphere where the assignment is introduced, discussed, and revised. But when students begin working on the assignment, they may have questions that they did not anticipate. For instance, a student may have thought that he or she understood what the assignment means when it says "analyze" the case study under consideration, but now that the student attempts the analysis, he or she has questions. These questions may be explained by the rubric, but the student isn't reading the rubric well—suggesting that the professor will need to help interpret the rubric even after it has been thoroughly explained in class. This ongoing discussion about the rubric does not negate the need for the rubric to be completed early in the entire writing process for a particular writing assignment, else students do not have the criteria at hand while working on the assignment that they and the professor will use to evaluate the assignment.

The process of grading students' writing for a particular assignment is continuous. Grading begins with the writing assignment, builds with the development of a rubric or some other instrument that can be used throughout the writing process as an anchor for standards, gathers force when students refer to the rubric during the writing process to match their writing with the criteria specified by the rubric, surges forth when students evaluate each other's writing using a rubric or some other technique, and spills over when the professor uses the rubric to evaluate students' writing either in concert with each student's self-assessment using the rubric or in relation to the process that preceded professorial evaluation. Continuous and interlinked evaluation of a writing assignment is, of course, an ideal, and a worthy ideal. How well it can be sustained over many years of teaching without appropriate administrative support in the form of funds for faculty development, appropriate class sizes, and teaching loads that allow professors to promote writing in their classes is an open question, but as an ideal, continuous and interlinked evaluation of a writing assignment is worth pursuing.

Teach students to conduct peer and self-evaluations

Some readers may have raised questions when I talked earlier about student peer evaluations, wondering, perhaps, whether peer evaluations are useful (particularly in light of research that says more expert evaluation by professors may not be very useful) and whether students have the necessary skills to evaluate their peers' writing. The queries are related. Peers can provide useful observations about how to improve a peer's writing (just as professors can provide useful observations), but one factor related to the usefulness of peers' comments is professorial management of the peer critiquing process, including training students to be effective peer evaluators (Bean, 1979; Carlson & Roellich, 1983; McKendy, 1990; Stewart, 1980; Thompson, 1981; Zhu, 1995). In other words, professors cannot assume that by putting students in groups and giving them a critique sheet of some sort that the students will make useful comments on a peer's writing. Nor can professors assume that a student writer will recognize useful comments on his or her writing and follow them when revising the draft. Nevertheless, these two problems do not negate professorial responsibility to manage peer critiques by providing instruction on how to critique, modeling peer critique before the entire class, assigning students to critique groups, ensuring that students have time to complete critiques, and insisting that students discuss their critiques with the person whose writing they evaluated.

Self-assessments are even trickier than peer assessments, as can be seen by the following story about self-assessment at a major research university in this country. The faculty at the university were asked to rank their performance as teachers in the top 25% of teachers on the campus, the next 25%, and so on. The results? Seventy-five percent of the professors ranked their teaching performance in the top 25% of the teachers on campus. The *self* in self-assessment may find it hard to evaluate one's own performance in relation to criteria. This finding is not surprising, particularly when professors realize that some students have learned to give themselves high evaluations because the professor will use that evaluation as the basis for a course grade, that honest and accurate self-criticism is hindered by blind spots a person may not even recognize as blind spots, and that some of the best students give themselves evaluations that demonstrate they have been overly severe in assessing their performance. Self-evaluation, therefore, should be anchored to criteria and should be checked against peers' and the teacher's evaluations so that students receive a composite picture of their performance from various angles (Beach, 1982; Beck, 1982; Chiseri-Strater, 1993; Kirby, 1987; Sandman, 1993).

Students' evaluations of themselves have two purposes. First, students can check their observations about their writing during the writing process with others' observations. Doing so can help students adjust their perceptions of what they are writing and provide information for revising their writing. Second, students can join with others at the end of the grading process to make a final decision about quality. Again, the student has the opportunity to compare his or her decision about quality with peers' and the professor's decisions.

A student can use the same evaluative technique, such as a rubric, as peers and professor use to evaluate his or her final performance. In fact, a rubric can have three columns that allow for evaluations by peers, self, and the professor and use the same criteria so that a student can see similarities and differences among the evaluators. These three evaluations do not have to have the same weight. A peer evaluation can count for 25% of the final grade, a self-evaluation can count for 25%, and the professor's evaluation can count for 50%. Such a distribution allows the professor to make corrections for whatever misperceptions he or she believes students have made in their final evaluations on which the grade will be based.

Although the grading process does have a terminus point, generally the grade, professors can extend the process by talking to students individually to explain any points of difference raised by the various evaluations. Professors might be uncomfortable about talking with students, especially those students who received a lower grade than they believe they deserve, but students do deserve the opportunity to find out why a professor rendered a particular judgment, especially when that judgment is out of sync with peers' evaluations and self-assessments. Professors can turn a student's disappointment with a grade into a writing task by asking the student to provide acceptable reasons in writing why the grade should be adjusted, if the student believes adjusting the grade is necessary. Professors also can submit the student's written work to another professor and ask that professor to adjudicate the grade. Doing so would require the other professor to evaluate the student's work without the benefit of the colleague's evaluation but with the benefit of the peer and self-assessments. If the other professor provides a higher evaluation than the one his or her colleague provided, the student is the beneficiary of the higher evaluation or can receive the mean of the two evaluations. If a penalty is attached to reevaluation by an outside expert, students who have a worthy complaint may not be willing to submit to outside reevaluation, so professors should note that the purpose of outside reevaluation is not to penalize students but to provide a means of redress for students who believe they have been evaluated unfairly. Of course, professors will want to limit this use of external evaluators for students who have widely different notions of what grade a paper should receive from the professor and peers. Otherwise, professors might find themselves out of favor with overworked colleagues.

Conduct student-professor conferences

Another way professors can encourage students to be engaged in the evaluative process is by conducting student-professor conferences. Student-professor conferences, in the formal sense, are one-on-one meetings between the student and professor outside the classroom. For instance, students sign up for 10- or 15-minute appointments to discuss their writing. Some professors simply convert class time into conference time so that during scheduled class time students sign up for a student-professor conference. This approach may not be practical in all circumstances, but a week of classes might profitably be used as conference time for one semester.

During conference time, the professor asks questions about the present state of a student's writing, generally a specific writing project the student is working on, and listens to students answer those questions. The professor's purpose is to give the student suggestions for revision, encourage the student to take responsibility for his or her writing, and provide the student with one person's reading of the student's writing.

> *Teacher/student talk is a powerful means by which we can make students aware of our willingness to assist them in becoming better writers. And by using talk to promote that social awareness that writers need, we are adding a powerful dimension to the writer's awareness of writing for others. Teacher/student talk is, then, that comfortable setting where writer and helper talk about—and work together on—a piece of writing.* (Harris, 1990, p. 160)

Literature on student-professor conferences notes that the purpose of the conference really is to create a conversation, not to give the professor an opportunity to talk on and on but to engage the student in a conversation about the student's writing.*

Informal student-professor evaluation includes conferring with a student briefly during class, listening to peer group activities and making comments about issues a particular paper raises, and talking with students after class to respond to questions they raise. Such informal evaluation sessions can be quite useful to students as they seek expert advice about their progress in writing.

*For specific instructions on how to conduct student-professor conferences, see Arbur, 1977; Beach, 1989; Carnicelli, 1980; Fassler, 1978; Harris, 1986; Memering, 1973; Rose, 1982).

Conclusion

Students should be part of the evaluative process because their involvement in that process has the potential to provide them with skills they will need to evaluate writing not only in academic but also in nonacademic settings. In addition, involving students in the evaluative process causes professors to be involved in the process in ways that they might not have been involved in before. Professors have to ensure that writing assignments are clear and cogent by testing the assignments with a class of students. Professors have to match evaluative criteria with writing assignments by providing evaluative instruments (such as a rubric) or evaluative opportunities (such as peer critiques).

PROVIDING FEEDBACK FOR REVISION: Reading and Responding to Students' Writing

A professor's purpose in providing feedback to students about a particular piece of writing should be to give them insight for revising that piece of writing. This purpose assumes that the professor provides feedback during the writing process and that any feedback the professor provides when giving a grade to a student's writing is not designed to help the student revise the writing. A grade is the last assessment of a student's writing, and any comments the professor makes when assigning a grade appear to be superfluous for purposes of revision.

Although professors may agree with the premise that feedback should give students help in revising their writing, professors' understanding of what constitutes useful feedback may in fact run counter to the purpose of providing useful feedback; thus, the first part of this discussion identifies three common uses of feedback that are not in accord with the purpose of revision. The second part, using the literature on feedback, explains why professors might have difficulties providing effective feedback, and the third gives advice about how professors can provide useful feedback that will help students revise their writing.

Common Misperceptions About Feedback

Three common misperceptions about feedback are that its primary purpose is to identify errors, justify a grade, and provide help over a range of writing assignments.

Feedback identifies errors

A professor may use feedback—reading and responding to a piece of writing—to identify errors. Although identifying errors can be incorporated into feedback designed for revision, identifying errors should not be the major purpose for providing feedback. The problem with limiting feedback to the identification of errors—particularly errors in grammar, mechanics, and spelling—is that correcting such errors may not have much to do with improving the substance of a student's writing. If, for instance, a student wrote a brilliant history paper littered with surface errors (errors in grammar, mechanics, and spelling), correcting those errors might be all that remains to make the paper a superior work. Such papers, however, are rare, because students who write brilliant papers generally have a good grasp of grammar, mechanics, and spelling. In fact, students' papers laden with surface errors also generally have problems in logic, sentence structure, and organization. To point out surface errors in such papers will do little to help the student revise the writing so that logic, sentence structure, and organization are corrected. In fact, focusing on surface errors does not help students become better writers, and "pointing out too many errors at once actually discourages writers from doing further revision" (Fulwiler, Gorman, & Gorman, 1986, p. 57). When professors respond only or primarily to students' writing by marking errors, students may come to believe that *not* making errors is what really matters in good writing. Moreover, if the preponderance of feedback the professor gives is identifying errors, students can perceive that the teacher's comments are editorial recommendations, and thus students will correct errors to receive a higher grade, assuming that correcting errors is all the teacher requires (Dohrer, 1991; Mitchell, 1994).

Another problem of professors' and students' fixation on errors is that students may not expand their writing repertoire because they want to play it safe when writing. Such an attitude of caution is inimical to the early stages of the writing process in which trial and error should be encouraged. When the avoidance of errors is uppermost in the hierarchy of writing values, the exploration of a topic is virtually eliminated, because exploration requires a willingness to chart new courses, discard inadequate ways of doing things, and try new methods that the student has not mastered. Error and exploration go hand in hand. If, however, students perceive of writing as reproducing on paper what they have compiled in their minds, then errors in transcription really are the major problem a writer faces. But the transcription view of writing is false, not in accord with the practices of all kinds of writers in various professions and contrary to the findings of modern composition theory. Fixation on errors—whether by students or professors—is detrimental to writing because it does not comport with a process approach to writing.

All of which is not to say that errors are unimportant. Professors need to tell students that errors are important because they can distract readers, provide a reason for readers to criticize the writer's competence, and cause ambiguity in communication. In addition, professors need to tell students that errors, such as pesky problems with spelling, commas, and apostrophes, will become a point of attention toward the end of the writing process but that students should not concentrate on errors early in the process.

Even so, the writing process allows writers to address various errors throughout the process. For instance, as students see more clearly what they want to say, they begin to fix sentences that are unclear, reorganize their arguments to make more sense, catch a lapse in spelling or punctuation, and so forth. Revising, then, includes identifying and correcting errors, but such identification and correction arise from the student's need to create a coherent text that he or she can understand, not from a preoccupation with error. Because a student's evolving text is quite fluid, some errors the student makes will vanish when a piece of text is discarded. The student will jettison a piece of text, including the comma splice the student didn't see, because the student believes that the text doesn't work in the evolving argument. Students may eliminate some errors unknowingly. Thus, identifying and correcting errors becomes a pragmatic concern for students as they see that something they wrote doesn't quite work and seek to mend it, either by fixing or cutting it.

Nevertheless, once the writer has worked through a series of drafts, the writing process includes a time for formal peer critique, a time when others can give a fresh look at the evolving text. "We all know how much easier it is to see problems in someone else's writing; what that suggests, of course, is that we have a critical distance here that we don't have from our own work" (Fulwiler, 1986, p. 31). This critical distance is one reason peer reviewers can be so helpful. After peer critiques, after more revisions, and as the due date for an assignment is approaching with urgency, the writing process includes a time for editing and proofreading, which is when the student and peer editor can concentrate on finding and eliminating any remaining errors.

Feedback justifies the grade

Professors also can provide feedback to students' writing to justify a grade. Actually, such response is not very useful in providing students with feedback for revision, because the grade is a terminal point in a writing assignment. Once a grade is administered, the writing assignment is finished. The comments a professor makes to justify a grade are evidence for the grade, not feedback for revision. The two ought not be confused.

Some professors might object by noting that giving a grade to a student and providing opportunity for revision so that the student can earn a higher grade do make such feedback useful for revision. Perhaps, but the focus has subtly shifted from fulfilling the conditions of the writing assignment to revising it for a better grade. Wouldn't it be better for professors to provide every possible opportunity (given the time constraints of the class) for students to revise their work so that the professor can thus reinforce the motivation to seek excellence in completing the writing assignment rather than foster a stick-and-carrot approach to writing by encouraging revision for a higher grade? In other words, promoting revision for the sake of a higher grade need not be done when students have every opportunity to revise for the sake of meeting the conditions of the assignment. Then a grade is final and need not be negotiated by asking the student to engage the hope of a higher grade, when, in fact, a higher grade may not be possible. If a student has been given ample opportunity to produce the best work possible up to that point, is it realistic to think that the student will be able to revise the paper sufficiently to make a significantly better grade? Will raising the grade from C– to C be satisfactory for the student or the professor? Will the time required for the student to revise and the professor to reevaluate the paper be justified?

Feedback for one assignment can be transferred to another assignment

Professors might argue that, even when feedback is juxtaposed with a grade, students can transfer the feedback on one writing assignment to the next writing assignment. Professors might believe, for instance, that if they explain to students on one paper how to solve a particular problem of organization or logic, the students will be able to transfer the solution for that problem to the next paper and other papers they write. This purpose for responding is loaded with assumptions that may not be true.

For instance, a solution to a problem in organization in one genre may not work in another genre. Solutions for narratives may not fit argumentative papers. Indeed, if a student is struggling with the requirements of a particular assignment, the student may even make mistakes he or she would not normally make because the student is preoccupied with the difficulty of satisfying new requirements. Or even when the professor repeatedly marks surface errors, a student may continue to make those errors, assignment after assignment. The student simply may not see that *it's* is not the same as *its,* no matter how many times the professor marks the error. In short, the assumption that a student will be able to transfer what he or she learned about revising on one assignment to what needs to be revised on another assignment remains an assumption and does not provide adequate grounds for mixing feedback with a grade.

Certainly, linking revision with a grade might be effective when the professor is teaching students how to perfect a particular type of writing. For instance, when the professor is teaching students how to write a progress report, gives students explicit directions about what a progress report contains, and constructs a series of assignments so that students write a variety of progress reports, then feedback on one progress report could have a salutary effect on students' preparation of subsequent progress reports. Students still may fail to grasp the difference between *its* and *it's,* however, so professors might want to deal with common errors by explaining why *its* and *it's* can be confused and providing students with a means to test their use of the two words.

After considering the difficulties associated with three common problems in providing feedback to students, a professor logically might ask, What constitutes useful feedback? The literature on feedback to students' writing gives two answers to that question. Negatively, the literature explains what not to do and why. This negative side of the literature is important to examine because it gives professors insights into why certain common practices are ineffective and sets the stage for the positive answer the literature offers—what professors can do to give useful feedback. First, let's look at the negative side of the literature.

Why Professors Might Have Difficulties Providing Effective Feedback

A major assumption I have criticized throughout this monograph is that professors, because of their formal authority, possess subject matter and teaching authority. This faulty assumption has lead to the assertion that because a professor has formal and subject matter authority, the professor automatically has teaching authority. If that were the case, then professors would know how to respond effectively to students' writing, because effective response to students' writing is a characteristic of teaching authority. Indeed, there would be no need for literature designed to train teachers of composition (of all people!) how to respond effectively to students' writing. Yet such literature is readily available (see, e.g., Connors & Glenn, 1992; Larson, 1986; Peterson, 1995; Tarvers, 1993). Not surprisingly then, the literature on professors' responses to students' writing calls into question the assertion that professors "just know" how to respond effectively to students' writing (Connors & Lunsford, 1993).

For example, professors say they are evaluating students' writing using criterion *x* but actually evaluate using criterion *y*, sending mixed messages to students (Kline, 1976). Professors may incorrectly question intent in students' writing, providing directives for revision that take control from students (Crowley, 1989; Heller, 1989; Welch, 1998) and diverting students from *their* intentions in writing (N. Sommers, 1982). Even the comments professors make may refute the advice they give, as, for example, when professors tell students "how important it is to write well" but write comments on students' compositions "suggest[ing] just the opposite" (Patterson, 1983, p. 178; see also S. Smith, 1997; Straub, 1996).

The way a professor reads students' writing is critically related to the way the professor evaluates students' writing.

In essence, the way a professor reads students' writing is critically related to the way the professor evaluates students' writing. Professors read students' writing using three overlapping personae: experiencer, examiner, and evaluator (Cowan, 1977). Then, in commenting on students' writing, professors send mixed messages to students because the professors have not distinguished among the personae. In reflecting on her reading of students' writing, Ede came to realize that the "natural, inevitable, and commonsensical" way she thought she read students' writing was really "complex and problematic" (1989, p. 156). Others have noted the problematic nature of the way professors read students' writing (Lawson & Ryan, 1989; Miller, 1984; Murray, 1989; Nold, 1978; Schwegler, 1991; Stewart, 1975; Zebroski, 1989). In short, professors neither read nor respond to students' writing the same way all the time. As professors, we give students a response to their writing based on *one* particular reading of that writing. And that one particular reading is not necessarily characteristic of the other particular readings our colleagues give when they respond to students' writing.

In addition, when students evaluate professors' responses to their writing, they raise questions about how effective those responses are (Lynch & Klemans, 1978; Whichard, Gamber, Lester, Leighton, Carlberg, & Whitaker, 1992). Indeed, students may not understand professors' comments in the way the professor intended the comments to be understood (Hiatt, 1975; Ziv, 1982). And it's slight consolation that although professors can give conflicting advice to students about students' writing, the impact of most professors' comments is negligible (Sloan, 1977). This observation may be too quick to exonerate professors' feedback, however, because such feedback may be harmful when professors mislabel errors or fail to identify them in students' writing (Greenbaum & Taylor, 1981).

These general observations about problems with professors' responses to students' writing are accompanied in the literature by specific responses that are not particularly helpful. Those specific responses can be grouped into three categories: cryptic responses, negative responses, and too much response.

Cryptic responses

Cryptic responses are either one-word comments (e.g., "awkward") or abrupt commands (e.g., "rewrite this"). I encountered such a cryptic response while working with a graduate student on his dissertation. The student's adviser had recommended that the student pay a professional to edit his dissertation, so the student called me. In the course of working with the student to help him revise his dissertation, I met with him after his adviser had responded to one of the chapters in the dissertation. Next to one paragraph, the professor had written in large letters, "revise." I asked the student what the professor wanted the student to revise. He said, "I don't know." I then asked the student whether he had asked the professor what needed to be revised in the paragraph. The student responded, "He told me just to revise it." Little wonder that the impact of one-word comments on students' papers can be limited (A. D. Cohen, 1987).

Students' responses to cryptic comments fall into two categories. When a student reads "revise" without any other direction, the student can either say, "I thought something was wrong with this passage, but I couldn't place my finger on it, and I still can't," or the student can say, "What's wrong with this passage? Seems OK to me!" Cryptic comments do not provide enough information for the student to revise according to specific directions. If the student does attempt to revise a passage based on a cryptic comment, the student has to make assumptions about whatever problem the professor believes is at issue but has not stated. The bald assertion "revise!" and the masked judgment "awkward!" are cryptic statements that do not provide students with adequate information about what needs to be revised. "Without specific directions for improvement, the student does not know where to begin" (Hahn, 1981, p. 10).

Negative responses

Another problem with professors' responses is that they tend to be negative (Daiker, 1989). Part of the reason for negative responses to students' writing may be that professors do not read students' writing the way they read other writing. Although professors do not read published texts with the intention of finding the type of errors that they find in students' writing, professors generally expect to find errors of various sorts when reading students' papers, so they look for errors—problems in logic, ill formed sentences, various surface errors. In essence, the professor compares students' writings with standards used to evaluate published texts. If true, it is unfortunate, because students' writings have not had the opportunity to go through the publishing process to the extent that published texts do. Students do not, for instance, have the privilege of consulting with a professional copy editor who labors intensively over a text to ensure that it is without spot or blemish. (Besides, such classroom consulting would be called plagiarism in many academic circles.) Students do not have the chance to review page proofs one last time before the text is published. So if students' writing is being evaluated on standards used to evaluate published writing, students ought to be given the same opportunities published authors, such as professors, have to create texts that can withstand the scrutiny of professional readers. When professors use the writing process in their classes, they give students many of the opportunities published authors have to create professional texts, but the level of care a published texts receives is, in most classrooms, still difficult to provide.

Another reason professors might make negative comments on students' writing could be frustration. While reading a batch of papers, the professor may become disheartened, realizing that the students did not do well in their attempts to fulfill the conditions of the writing assignment. The problem may be that the writing assignment was faulty or that the students were not given enough time to complete the assignment or that instructions were insufficient. Nevertheless, a professor might believe that the problems with poor writing rest with students and begin to make negative comments on their papers: "Who in the world would believe something like this? Only a moron"; "This is a stupid thing to say"; "Dumb idea"; "Didn't you complete freshman composition?"; "Your poor writing ability suggests that you shouldn't be in college"; and so on. Such comments are not very useful in helping students revise their work and put the professor in a poor light, suggesting that he or she is not willing to help students improve but instead wants to demean students.

To counter any tendency to make unprofessional negative comments, professors can do two things. First, they can determine whether their pedagogy is a problem in helping students fulfill the writing assignment. Advice earlier in this monograph on developing a writing assignment can be consulted to check the clarity of a writing assignment. Even an excellent writing assignment, however, can be hindered by a pedagogy that does not lay out the writing process for students and identify checkpoints at which the professor will answer questions, ask students to produce drafts, and allow for peer review and self-evaluation. Second, professors may have to realign their preconceptions about what students *should* be able to do with what they can do. If most students in a class are not producing writing at a level of quality the professor believes is acceptable, then the problem may be the level of quality the professor has established. Sometimes, for instance, professors judge freshman students' writing on measures of quality that more properly apply to graduate students' writing. Admittedly, the problem of standards is sticky, but if students en masse are not meeting the standards of quality a professor establishes, something appears to be out of sync, and the professor's standards should not be immune from consideration as a potential problem.

Professors' negative responses to students' writing suggest that professors may have difficulty praising students' writing. The literature confirms this idea, noting that praise is a rare commodity in professors' responses to students' writing. Perhaps professors believe that only the best papers deserve praise or that students will mistake praise of some parts of the paper for an endorsement of the entire paper or that students should be mature enough to accept genuine criticism that is not laced with the palliative of praise. Genuine praise has an important affective impact on writers, however. "Writing to people who care about us—or what we have to say—engages us as writers more than writing to people who read our work in order to grade us" (Fulwiler, 1986, p. 25). When professors do not praise students for what is good in their writing, professors can discourage students from wanting to revise their writing and perhaps from wanting to write much at all. Students like both positive and negative comments, but a paper with mostly negative comments can be depressing (Reed & Burton, 1985).

When professors do not praise students for what is good in their writing, they can discourage students from wanting to revise their writing and perhaps from wanting to write much at all.

Too much response

Yet another problem the literature on response to students' writing identifies is too much response. Professors might think that they are doing a great service to students by writing comments on a student's paper that exceed the amount of text the student wrote. Although the impulse behind such a practice may be based on noble intentions and a keen sense of professional responsibility, the practice can be quite ineffective because students can be overwhelmed by too much response, wondering, "Where do I start in revising this paper?"

The problem with too much response is that it tends to be diffuse and unfocused. If, after reading all that a professor has written, the student is left wondering where to begin in revising his or her paper, the problem may be that the professor has provided too much response.

How Professors Can Provide Useful Feedback

Difficulties professors might have in providing useful responses to students' writing point to ways professors can provide useful feedback. At the very least, we can learn from unhelpful responses that professors can provide useful feedback to help students revise their work—detailed, focused responses that include praise. More can and should be said, however, about how professors can provide helpful feedback, including differences in professors' and students' perspectives when they read a text, pointers for reading text aloud, pointers on how to write marginal comments, and pointers on how to write terminal comments.

Differences in professors' and students' perspectives when they read a text

When providing feedback on students' writing, professors need to keep in mind that students may read a text differently from the way a professor reads a text. Professors have been trained to read texts in certain ways, particularly regarding disciplinary conventions and rhetorical arguments. Students, however, are apprentices, learning how to read history, philosophy, psychology, and sociology texts—perhaps all in one semester. As apprentices, students need to be taught how to read texts in particular disciplines and how to write texts for those disciplines. The professor cannot assume that just because students have completed their writing requirement for general education they can write an acceptable paper for any discipline. Rather, professors might want to take the position that students are *not* prepared to write an acceptable paper when they walk into class the first day, not because the students are mentally deficient, but because they are untrained in disciplinary conventions.

The professor also might find it helpful to recognize that students are much more willing than professors are to read a paper with a generous attitude, filling in gaps the writer left (Newkirk, 1984). One consequence of this generous approach to reading is that students may not understand why a professor is asking for more detail or pointing out a gap when, from a student's perspective, the reader bridges that gap by supplying what the author obviously intended but didn't state.

Another problem with reading professors may want to consider is differences in students' gender. A woman may not write according to male patterns of written communication, and professors might want to acknowledge that a female (or male) approach to writing should not disallow a male (or female) approach. The recognition of different approaches to writing based on gender may not be apparent at first when professors investigate it, but literature on those differences should sound a caution to professors who believe that "good writing is good writing" without considering the impact of gender on how one defines good writing (Ballard & Clanchy, 1991; Barnes, 1990; E. Flynn, 1989; J. Flynn, 1989; Gabriel, 1990; Haswell & Tedesco, 1991; Stygall et al., 1994).

When professors are aware of differences in the ways they read a text and the ways students read texts, professors can begin to respond to students' writing by reading an example of a student's writing out loud to a class and explaining how they interpret the text. For instance, a professor can select a text a student wrote the previous year to fulfill an assignment, mask the student's name, and make an overhead of the text. The professor then reads part of the text, perhaps the first paragraph, and explains what works and what doesn't.

In using students' writing in class, I have found particularly bad examples are useful in helping students learn how to read a resume, for instance. Students begin to see what doesn't work and why. I use a series of graduated examples so that bad examples lead to better examples that in turn lead to good examples. The purpose is to show students how to read a text so that they formulate principles of text interpretation they can use when they revise their own work and evaluate their peers' writing.

Speaking comments on students' papers

One way to continue oral instruction for revision is "cassette grading" (Carson & McTasney, 1973; Hays, 1978; Hurst, 1975; Olsen, 1982), in which the professor records his or her comments on students' papers by using a cassette player. One of the virtues of cassette grading is that students hear the professor responding to the text extemporaneously or with some cues from a text the professor has already marked. Such response can have an immediacy and an authenticity that may be hard to capture in other ways.

Writing comments on students' papers

Commonly, however, professors respond with written comments about students' writing with the purpose of providing advice and direction so that students can revise their papers. It is vital to note at the outset of this discussion on written comments, however, that professors have latitude in the way they write comments. For instance, after analyzing the written comments of 12 composition scholars on a set of student papers, Straub and Lunsford (1995) found that the scholars used different styles in making written comments: authoritative, directive, advisory, Socratic, dialectic, and analytical. Thus, no one style can account for the various types of helpful responses professors can make about students' writing. The following guidelines, offered in part as a counterbalance to the negative approaches cited in the literature on responding, may be useful to professors who are wondering how to make effective written responses to students' writing.

- *Create a dialogue when writing responses, particularly marginal responses.* Show students how to read a paper from a professor's viewpoint. For instance, a professor can ask questions ("How can a person who believes in theism explain the geological evidence that seems to contradict theistic claims?"), make observations ("I don't understand how a person, such as the one you are using as an example in your paper, can say that circular reasoning is normative and then appeal to evidence as a way for people to determine what is true."), pose possibilities ("I agree that people should have concern for their neighbors, but what if my neighbor does destructive things, including harming my loved ones? How would the principle of altruism you are recommending allow me to deal with my neighbor?"), and ask for clarification ("How exactly are you defining the word *vicarious?").* The purpose of creating a dialogue with students is to help them see how a person who thinks critically about things responds to a text so that they can revise their writing to answer the questions the critical thinker poses. Evaluation should be "an open-ended transaction with the student writer rather than a final pronouncement of merit on the student's writing" (Diogenes, Roen, & Moneyhun, 1986, p. 61).
- *Point out successes.* Let students know when something they wrote works—which does not mean that the professor is obligated to praise students for every comma properly used. It does not even mean that professors need to balance praise with other comments. Rather, it means that a word of encouragement, judiciously placed, may motivate a student to see the value of revisions. Something of value can be improved while something of little value may not be worth the effort needed to add value. Although praiseworthy grading (Dragga, 1985, 1988; Zak, 1990) focuses on an almost exclusive use of praise, students need more than encouragement. They need specific direction for revising their papers.
- *Refrain from making unprofessional comments.* "Responses manifesting scorn, hostility, condescension, flippancy, superficiality, or boredom are always out of line"

(Hovarth, 1984, p. 142). Such responses are out of line because they are unprofessional. Although a professor might make snide comments about a colleague in a book review of the colleague's work or take potshots at colleagues who hold to theoretical views that are at variance with the professor's, such responses are inappropriate when professors mentor students during the writing and grading processes. While a purpose of those processes is to indoctrinate students into disciplinary conventions, the professor is not obligated to treat students with the disdain that may be typical of an academic discipline.

- *Summarize.* In making comments at the end of a student's paper, the professor can summarize the gist of the marginal comments, providing students more specific direction for revising. A professor might recommend that a student consider doing *x, y,* and *z* to reorganize the paper, develop a particular point more fully and relate it to the other points in the paper, consider the relationship between parts A and B of the paper, and write a section that shows how the two relate, and so on. The terminal comment is a time when the professor can summarize his or her response to the paper.
- *Give students options.* Students want to know which comments they need to take seriously. This approach to the professor's comments is problematic, because students are asking for a recipe. The professor can help students move beyond the recipe approach by giving one or two suggestions for dealing with a problem. Professors can write, "If you want to take direction *x* in revising your paper, then you might consider focusing on *y*. However, if you want to take direction O in revising your paper, then you might consider focusing on P." In other words, professors should give students options, not mandates, for revising.
- *Write comments that model good writing.* Yes, professors' comments on students' papers fall into the category of a rough draft. Nevertheless, professors can model good writing by making clear and cogent comments, which does not mean that the comments will be free of errors. Professors should explain to students that professors' comments are rough draft material, liable to all the foibles and follies of unedited comments. Nevertheless, the substance of the comments should be models of effective communication.

- *Defer assigning a grade as long as possible.* A grade ends a writing assignment and may not be much help in giving students substantive feedback about the quality of their writing. So the professor might consider focusing on the writing and grading processes as long as possible before bringing them to closure. Deferring grades should not be an excuse for waiting until the last moment to inform students that they are failing. Rather, professors who defer grades should provide students with feedback about their writing and give them some provisional idea of how they are doing, say at least C-level work or below.

The appendix provides an example of how effective techniques can be used to respond to a student's paper.

Conclusion

Providing students with feedback so that they can revise their work effectively is a hard job, requiring a professional and compassionate reading of students' writing. Examples of the negative responses cited in this section serve as a caution so that professors will refrain from giving feedback that will not help students revise their work. Examples of positive responses and guidelines for making positive responses serve as aids the professor can use to perfect the art of providing positive feedback to students. One way to gauge the effectiveness of feedback from professors is improvement in the drafts students produce guided by a professor's responses. When students do revise their writing based on a professor's feedback to produce better drafts, the professor can experience a great deal of satisfaction, knowing that students took to heart at least some of the professor's suggestions for revision and produced praiseworthy papers.

CONCLUSION AND RECOMMENDATIONS

While writing this book, I was called to serve as a member of the university Grade Appeal Committee; that experience as a committee member provides a fitting conclusion to this book. Student P, a graduate student, and Professor Q were the combatants in the appeal. Student P alleged that Professor Q had never provided a syllabus at the beginning of the course, had not determined until late in the course what written product the student would need to produce (which turned out to be a research paper), and had never given a written evaluation of the student's research paper. Professor Q confirmed Student P's complaint regarding those three points. In defending herself, however, Professor Q stated that graduate students should know what is expected of them and that a professor's job is not to baby-sit graduate students. Thus, Professor Q never required drafts of the research paper and did not mark the final research paper, noting that a colleague had said not to mark final drafts of students' papers because comments at that point aren't useful for revising a paper. Professor Q, in making closing remarks to the committee, wondered whether her standards were too high.

Two points strike me about Professor Q's defense. First, Professor Q failed to give adequate guidance to the graduate student. The committee, comprising professors and graduate students, unanimously agreed about that point. Professor Q did not explain to the student what was required for a particular grade in the course and how the student's performance would be evaluated. Certainly, at the end of the course when the student turned in a research paper, Professor Q did apply standards to grade the paper, but those standards were in Professor Q's head. Student P did not have access to those standards during the writing process. Professor Q also misunderstood collegial advice about not marking students' final drafts, because Professor Q took those comments out of context. Indeed, Professor Q, although a recipient of training in writing across the curriculum (in which the writing process was thoroughly discussed), failed to put into context advice about *when* to provide written feedback on students' writing, and took a piece of advice about not providing written comments on final drafts without taking all the advice about shepherding students through the *entire* writing process.

Second, Professor Q made assumptions about students' ability that were not based on accurate information. That graduate students *should* be able to work independently without significant supervision by the professor is an assumption, often based on an elitist view of graduate education. The central issue, however, is not whether graduate students should be able to work independently; they should. The central issue is how professors can teach graduate students to work independently.

Professor Q's attitude toward graduate students is echoed by professors who teach undergraduates: Students *should* know how to do thus and thus. Unfortunately, professors' expectations of what students should know and be able to do may not match the reality of what students do know and are able to do. When this mismatch of expectations and reality collides, professors have two options. They can criticize students and give them the low grades they deserve because they are ill prepared to do college-level work, or they can use their authorities—formal, subject matter, and teaching—to help students achieve the next level or levels of knowledge and skill they need to be successful within and without the academy. The first option, it appears, is little more than an abdication of professional responsibility. The second requires professors to avail themselves of opportunities for faculty development so they can enrich their teaching authority. The writing and grading processes, intertwined as they are, provide professors with tools that can enrich their teaching authority, enabling them to enable students.

The writing and grading processes, intertwined as they are, provide professors with tools that can enrich their teaching authority, enabling them to enable students.

In light of the enormous literature on grading students' classroom writing, the following recommendations are offered:

1. *Professors should consider tailoring the writing and grading processes to their particular classroom situations if they want students to learn how to perform well as writers.* The writing and grading processes do not guarantee students' success in writing; rather, they provide a framework for enabling students to learn how to approach a writing task. Therefore, the processes are not a panacea for writing ills. Some students may need help with writing difficulties—such as blocks to writing that require professional counseling—that a professor cannot provide. Nevertheless, the writing and grading processes provide professor and students with a proven method of teaching and learning about writing.
2. *Professors who have not included much writing in their classes might consider using more writing as a way to*

help students learn. Writing is not transferring a text in a writer's mind to a piece of paper using a pen or a keyboard, but a way to work through problems to determine how they might be solved. Writing is a way of making thinking visible. First, students learn to create writer-centered documents designed to help them find out what they are saying. Second, students learn to revise those documents into reader-centered works that communicate to audiences what the students have learned. Writing, therefore, can be an invaluable tool in helping students learn and then transform that learning into information others can use to learn.

3. *Professors should not grade all writing.* Although the focus of this monograph is on the grading process, culminating in a grade, professors are not obligated to read or to grade every piece of writing students produce. For example, I use "exit slips" in many of my classes. At the end of each class, students, before leaving, write about five lines on a slip of paper to tell me their thoughts and feelings about the class that day. The exit slips are anonymous. I read the slips to get immediate feedback about the class, to glean questions students may have and that I need to answer next class period, to get a sense of possible frustrations or problems I need to address, and to enjoy positive comments about the class. I put the exit slips in a pile the next class and ask students to retrieve their slip. I neither mark nor grade the exit slips, but so many exit slips equals 5 or 10% of a student's grade.
4. *Professors should consider carefully the time required to use the writing and grading processes.* It's probably quite clear, if a reader has read from the beginning of the monograph until this point, that the effective use of writing in the classroom for any significant writing assignment requires lots of time in preplanning, in administering the writing and grading processes, and in determining the effectiveness of those processes so that the professor can make adjustments the next time around. Frankly, the time may not be worth the effort if sufficient support is not available. If a professor teaches 4 classes of 30 students each semester, it would require a superhuman effort to use the writing and grading processes regularly in all those classes throughout the se-

mester. The professor who expends such effort will become a good candidate for burnout—and possibly come to the point of rejecting the processes as unrealistic. Therefore, I recommend that professors with heavy teaching loads consider using the processes judiciously, perhaps asking students in each class to go through the entwined processes for one major writing assignment. It is better to use the processes effectively in a limited way than not use them at all. And professors are in the best position to determine when the processes should be used for their classes.

5. *Professors might consider integrating literature on grading into their professional reading schedule.* Those who read this monograph have acquired an introduction to the literature on grading, but they should realize that a host of sources are available on grading students' classroom writing. The reference list includes some of those sources. The literature on grading is not static, however, and new books and articles on grading continue to be published. The journals and book publishers listed in the bibliography regularly produce literature on classroom grading; professors can consult current issues of those journals and catalogs to keep abreast of the latest literature on grading classroom writing.

APPENDIX: Example of a Student's Paper With Effective Written Comments

Fiber and it's Amazing Benefits

Introduction

Fiber has amazing benefits when added to our diet. But what is fiber? Fiber is "the 'skeleton' of all plants. If plants did not have fiber, they would collapse like jelly. Fiber is the wall of all plant cells. The nourishment is inside; the fiber is the wall."[1] So perhaps you already see a problem with taking fiber out of our diet. If the nourishment is inside the fiber of wall and we take out the fiber then we also take out all the "good stuff." I wonder why we cheat ourselves out of the health benefits. As I read more and more on fiber I was surprised at all the things it does for the body. I really didn't think fiber did us so much good, but after reading about it, I realized what an active, important role it does play in our health. In fact, it has spurred me into making some dietary changes in my own life. I am now conscious about eating more fiber than I used to be. You can get fiber from many different foods. Nuts, beans, most fruits and vegetables, and whole grains contain fiber. The difficult thing is to eat enough of these fiber-rich foods. It is my hope that you will see through reading this paper that getting enough fiber is worth working on.

Reasons Why People Historically Stopped Eating Fiber

How did we come to cane in our eating of fiber? Regretion in the use of fiber goes back even to the ancient world some 3,000 years ago. From drawings inside the pyramids we find that for the ancient Egyptians baking bread was a common part of their activities. The Egyptians experimented with different kinds of soft wheat that could be milled to make a more refined bread than the usual bread produced by using hard wheat flour. The Greeks as far back as 330 BC and the first century Romans also made a distinction between lighter bread and darker, heavier bread. In Rome, the color of one's bread was an indicator of ones place in society. The darker one's bread the lower one's position in the Roman World. And history continues this theme. Man was continually trying to make a light, refined flour to bake white bread. In our society, it looks as though we have succeeded. We have also suffered health wise because of it.

Consequences

Because we don't everyday see dramatically how the elimination of fiber in our diet is progressively hurting us, we tend not to yield to change. But you will see from what fiber does to help prevent certain health problems that a lot of these problems could have been decreased in change had fiber been more active in the diet. I am not saying that by getting your daily dose of fiber that you are free from any illnesses. No one thing can preserve our health. You could eat the recommended amount of daily fiber and still die of a heart attack or get cancer. I am just concentrating on fiber and how its benefits can enrich your health. I believe this is the point Martin Katahn is making, when he says "When we try to pull out the essential protective dietary component in laboratory research, the results are confusing. The key ingredients seem to vary. Sometimes, as in the case of cancer, the key ingredient seems to be fiber, or vitamin A, or beta-carotene, or some other form of carotene, or vitamin E, or vitamin C, and so on............. there are many unknown substances in the foods we eat that may offer the protection, and not just the known vitamins, minerals, or fiber, so we are not sure just where to look."[2] Since health is obtained partly by nutrients working together fiber contributes to your health. And, as with most things, too much of a good thing is bad. Moderation is essential to health. Rather than focus on the negative, I will focus on the positive aspects, rewards, and benefits of getting enough fiber.

Benefits

One of the most obvious dietary problems that fiber takes care of is **constipation**. Fiber has the ability to bind things together namely bile and cholesterol. So another thing that fiber does is to help **lower your cholesterol level**. Medical research has proven that if you have a high cholesterol level you are more prone to heart diseases and certain cancers. If you get adequate amounts of fiber, therefore, you are less likely to be a victim of **heart diseases**, and fiber also **decreases the chance of certain cancers, the main one being colon cancer**. Fiber plays a major role in preventing **obesity**. After you eat it fiber expands in your stomach giving you a full sensation thus warding off overeating.

Fiber also takes a longer to digest than most foods staying in your stomach longer that most foods and making you feel full for a longer time. Obesity is a factor that contributes to diabetes. You could therefore say that fiber, in a round about way, **helps prevent diabetes**. In addition fiber also **helps prevent and alleviate hemorrhoids, helps prevent appendicitis and divericulosis**. Increasing your fiber intake provides many more "hidden" benefits than just the ones mentioned above. Eating foods that contain fiber provide numerous health benefits and prevents numerous illnesses besides those which fiber is connected in preventing. Vegetables and fruits that contain fiber also provide the body with needed vitamins and minerals. Hopefully now you see why fiber is an important ingredient to your health. I would now like to suggest some practical applications that you can use to make getting enough fiber a convenient, easy thing to do.

could you include this sentence with the previous sentence about overeating?

I wonder how fiber prevents these?

Are these two sentences saying the same thing?

I listed

In addition,

I hope that

Applications

According to the American Dietary Association (ADA) the average person should intake 20-35 grams of fiber daily. So allow me to make a few suggestions on how to get the recomended amount. One simple way to increase your fiber intake is to use whole-wheat flour in your cooking. You can find whole-wheat flour in most health-food stores. Some grocery stores carry fiber bars you can eat to boost you fiber intake. And one last suggestion that is a very convenient way to get fiber is to take fiber supplements. I hope some of these suggestions will inspire you to make some sort of decision to get your adequate fiber intake.

I see that I need 20-35 grams of fiber daily, but I don't see how I can get that amount by following your suggestions. For instance, how many fiber bars could I eat to get my daily fiber intake?

Could you give examples of fiber supplements?

---

[1] *Basic Care Bulletin* 2, Medical Training Institute of America.

Do you have a date or place of publication for this reference?

[2] Katahn, Martin. *One Meal At A Time.* NY, New York: W.W. Norton, 1991.

This is quite an improvement from your previous draft, and I can see that you have placed more emphasis on helping your audience understand your topic.

I'm looking forward to reading your next draft. If you stop by my office we can talk about the comments I've made and discuss the topic for your next paper.

REFERENCES

The Educational Resources Information Center (ERIC) Clearinghouse on Higher Education abstracts and indexes the current literature on higher education for inclusion in ERIC's database and announcement in ERIC's monthly bibliographic journal, *Resources in Education* (RIE). Most of these publications are available through the ERIC Document Reproduction Service (EDRS). For publications cited in this bibliography that are available from EDRS, ordering number and price code are included. Readers who wish to order a publication should write to the ERIC Document Reproduction Service, 7420 Fullerton Road, Suite 110, Springfield, Virginia 22153-2852. (Phone orders with VISA or MasterCard are taken at (800) 443-ERIC or (703) 440-1400.) When ordering, please specify the document (ED) number. Documents are available as noted in microfiche (MF) and paper copy (PC). If you have the price code ready when you call, EDRS can quote an exact price. The last page of the latest issue of *Resources in Education* also has the current cost, listed by code.

Agnew, E. (1995). Rigorous grading does not raise standards: It only lowers grades. *Assessing Writing, 2*(1), 91-103.

Allison, L., Bryant, L., & Hourigan, M. (Eds.) (1997). *Grading in the postprocess classroom*. Portsmouth, NH: Boynton/Cook.

Anderson, R. S., & Speck, B. W. (Eds.). (1998). *Changing the way we grade student performance: Classroom assessment and the new learning paradigm*. New Directions for Teaching and Learning No. 74. San Francisco: Jossey-Bass.

Andrews, J. D., & Sigband, N. B. (1984). How effectively does the "new" accountant communicate? Perceptions by practitioners and academics. *Journal of Business Communication, 21,* 18.

Angelo, T. A., & Cross, K. P. (1993). *Classroom assessment techniques: A handbook for college teachers* (2nd ed.). San Francisco: Jossey-Bass.

Anson, C., Brady, L., & Larson, M. (1993). Collaboration in practice. *Writing on the Edge, 4*(2), 80-96.

Anson, C. M., Schwiebert, J. E., & Williamson, M. M. (1993). *Writing across the curriculum: An annotated bibliography.* Westport, CT: Greenwood.

Arbur, R. (1977). The student-teacher conference. *College Composition and Communication, 28,* 338-342.

Ashton-Jones, E., & Thomas, D. K. (1990). Composition, collaboration, and women's ways of knowing: A conversation with Mary Belenky. *Journal of Advanced Composition, 10*(2): 275-292.

Ballard, B., & Clanchy, J. (1991). Assessment by misconception: Cultural influence and intellectual traditions. In L. Hamp-Lyons

(Ed.), *Assessing second language writing in academic contexts* (pp. 19-36). Norwood, NJ: Ablex.

Banta, T. W., Lund, J. P., Black, K. E., & Oblander, F. W. (1996). *Assessment in practice: Putting principles to work on college campuses*. San Francisco: Jossey-Bass.

Barnes, L. L. (1990). Gender bias in teachers' written comments. In S. L. Gabriel & I. Smithson (Eds.), *Gender in the classroom: Power and pedagogy* (pp. 140-159). Urbana, IL: University of Illinois Press.

Bazerman, C. (1983). Scientific writing as a social act: A review of the literature of the sociology of science. In P. V. Anderson, R. J. Brockmann, & C. R. Miller (Eds.), *New essays in technical and scientific communication: Research, theory, practice* (pp. 156-184). Farmingdale, NY: Baywood.

Beach, R. (1982). The pragmatics of self-assessing. In R. A. Sudol (Ed.), *Revising: New essays for teachers of writing* (pp. 71-83). Urbana, IL: National Council of Teachers of English.

Beach, R. (1989). Showing students how to assess: Demonstrating techniques for response in the writing conference. In C. M. Anson (Ed)., *Writing and response: Theory, practice, and research* (pp. 127-148). Urbana, IL: National Council of Teachers of English.

Beale, W. H., & King, D. W. (1981). A grading contract that works. *Exercise Exchange, 26*(1), 17-20.

Bean, J. C. (1979). A method of peer evaluation of student writing. *College Composition and Communication, 30,* 301-302.

Beck, J. P. (1982). Asking students to annotate their own papers. *College Composition and Communication, 33,* 322-326.

Belanger, J. (1985). Conflict between mentor and judge: Being fair and being helpful in composition evaluation. *English Quarterly, 18*(4), 79-92.

Belanoff, P. (1991). The myths of assessment. *Journal of Basic Writing, 10*(1), 54-66.

Belanoff, P. A. (1996). Portfolios: The good, the bad, and the beautiful. In R. Calfee & P. Perfumo (Eds.), *Writing portfolios in the classroom: Policy and practice, promise and peril* (pp. 349-358). Mahwah, NJ: Erlbaum.

Bendixen, A. (1986, April 27). It was a mess: How Henry James and others actually wrote a novel. *New York Times Book Review, 3,* 28-29.

Bishop, W. (1989). Qualitative evaluation and the conversational writing classroom. *Journal of Teaching Writing, 8,* 267-285.

Bleich, D. (1992, Spring). Evaluation, self-evaluation, and individualism. *ADE Bulletin* (no. 101), 9-14.

Bleich, D. (1997). What can be done about grading? In L. Allison, L. Bryant, & M. Hourigan (Eds.), *Grading in the post-process classroom: From theory to process* (pp. 15-35). Portsmouth, NH: Boynton/Cook.

Blinderman, A. (1970). Grade beans, not themes. *English Education, 1*(3), 159-165.

Blok, H. (1985). Estimating the reliability, validity, and invalidity of essay ratings. *Journal of Educational Measurement, 22*(1), 41-52.

Bloom, L. Z. (1997). Why I (used to) hate to give grades. *College Composition and Communication, 48,* 360-371.

Bonetti, K. (1988). An interview with Louise Erdich and Michael Dorris. *Missouri Review, 11*(2), 79-99.

Boss, R. S. (1988). *Formative evaluation of college composition: A formula for revision and grading*. ED 289 554. 31 pp. MF–01; PC–02.

Boss, R. S. (1989). *Application of performance appraisal systems to evaluation of college composition*. ED 313 090. 37 pp. MF–01; PC–02.

Bowman, J. P. (1973). Problems of the grading differential. *Journal of Business Communication, 11*(1), 22-30.

Brannon, L., & Knoblauch, C. H. (1982). On students' rights to their own texts: A model of teacher response. *College Composition and Communication, 33,* 157-166.

Brodkey, L. (1987). *Academic writing as social practice*. Philadelphia: Temple University Press.

Bryant, W. H. (1975). On grading composition objectively. *Canadian Modern Language Review, 31,* 260-263.

Buchholz, W. J. (1979). Behavioral evaluation: The checkmark grading system. *College Composition and Communication, 30,* 302-305.

Busching, B. (1998). Grading inquiry projects. In R. S. Anderson & B. W. Speck (Eds.), *Changing the way we grade student performance: Classroom assessment and the new learning paradigm* (pp. 89-96). New Directions for Teaching and Learning No. 74. San Francisco: Jossey-Bass.

Cameron, T. D. (1993). A responsible evaluation instrument and its impact on a developmental writing program. *Teaching English in the Two-Year College, 20,* 313-323.

Carlson, D. M., & Roellich, C. (1983, Spring). *Teaching writing easily and effectively to get results: Part II. The evaluation process*. Paper presented at the annual meeting of the National Council of Teachers of English, Seattle, WA. ED 233 372. 21 pp. MF–01; PC–01.

Carnicelli, T. A. (1980). The writing conference: A one-to-one conversation. In T. R. Donovan & B. W. McClelland (Eds.), *Eight approaches to teaching composition* (pp. 101-131). Urbana, IL: National Council of Teachers of English.

Carson, D. L., & McTasney, J. B. (1973). Grading technical reports with the cassette tape recorder: The results of a test program at the United States Air Force Academy. *Journal of Technical Writing and Communication, 3*(2), 131-144.

Charnley, M. V. (1978). Grading standards vary considerably, experiment shows. *Journalism Educator, 33*(3), 49-50.

Chiseri-Strater, E. (1993). Evaluation as acts of reading, response, and reflection. In T. Newkirk (Ed.), *Nuts and bolts: A practical guide to teaching college composition* (pp. 179-202). Portsmouth, NH: Boynton/Cook.

Christian, B. (1993, December). Freshman composition portfolios in a small college. *Teaching English in the Two-Year College,* 289-297.

Cohen, A. D. (1987). Student processing of feedback on their compositions. In A. Wenden & J. Rubin (Eds.), *Learner strategies in language learning* (pp. 57-69). New York: Oxford University Press.

Cohen, A. M. (1973). Assessing college students' ability to write compositions. *Research in the Teaching of English, 7,* 356-371.

Collison, M. C. (1974). No such word as *fail:* Presenting a pass–no credit grading plan within a traditional system. *California English Journal, 10*(2), 17-20.

Connors, R., & Glenn, C. (1992). Responding to and evaluating students' essays. In *The St. Martin's guide to teaching and writing* (pp. 89-107). New York: St. Martin's Press.

Connors, R. J., & Lunsford, A. A. (1993). Teachers' rhetorical comments on student papers. *College Composition and Communication, 44,* 200-223.

Cowan, G. (1977). The rhetorician's personae. *College Composition and Communication, 28,* 259-262.

Cripe, D. (1980). If grading makes you—GROUCHY—A system that works. *Scholastic Editor, 6*(1), 30-31.

Crowley, S. (1989). On intention in student texts. In B. Lawson, S. S. Ryan, & W. R. Winterowd (Eds.), *Encountering student texts: Interpretive issues in reading student writing* (pp. 99-110). Urbana, IL: National Council of Teachers of English.

Daiker, D. A. (1989). Learning to praise. In C. M. Anson (Ed.), *Writing and response: Theory, practice, and research* (pp. 103-113). Urbana, IL: National Council of Teachers of English.

Dautermann, J. (1993). Negotiating meaning in a hospital discourse community. In R. Spilka (Ed.), *Writing in the workplace: New research perspectives* (pp. 98-110). Carbondale, IL: Southern Illinois University Press.

Delworth, U. (1973). The contract system: Students as participants in the grading process. *Journal of College Student Personnel, 14,* 277.

Denman, M. E. (1978). The measure of success in writing. *College Composition and Communication, 29,* 42-46.

Dickey, J. (1978). A contract plan for teaching business communications. In G. H. Douglas (Ed.), *The teaching of business communication* (pp. 87-92). Champaign, IL: American Business Communication Association.

Diogenes, M., Roen, D. H., & Moneyhun, C. (1986). Transactional evaluation: The right question at the right time. *Journal of Teaching Writing, 5*(1), 59-70.

Dohrer, G. (1991). Do teachers' comments on students' papers help? *College Teaching, 39*(2), 48-54.

Dorazio, P. A. (1984). Teaching composition: A way to improve it. *Community College Review, 12*(2), 29-31.

Dragga, S. (1985). Praiseworthy grading. *Journal of Teaching Writing, 4*(2), 264-268.

Dragga, S. (1988). The effects of praiseworthy grading on students and teachers. *Journal of Teaching Writing, 7*(1), 41-50.

Dreyer, J. 1977. Grading student compositions: An alternative to the traditional weaponry. *Media & Methods, 13*(7), 62-64.

Duke, C. R. (1980). *An approach to revision and evaluation of student writing.* Paper presented at the annual meeting of the Conference on College Composition and Communication, Washington, DC. ED 188 167. 10 pp. MF–01; PC–01.

Dulek, R., & Shelby, A. (1981). Varying evaluative criteria: A factor in differential grading. *Journal of Business Communication, 18*(2), 41-50.

Ede, L. (1980). Audiences, paradigms, role playing, and evaluation: Some implications. *Kansas English, 65,* 8-10.

Ede, L. (1989). On writing reading and reading writing. In B. Lawson, S. S. Ryan, & W. R. Winterowd (Eds.), *Encountering student texts: Interpretive issues in reading student writing* (pp. 145-157). Urbana, IL: National Council of Teachers of English.

Ede, L., & Lunsford, A. (1984). Audience addressed/audience invoked: The role of audience in composition theory and pedagogy. *College Composition and Communication, 35,* 155-171.

Elbow, P. (1973). *Writing without teachers.* New York: Oxford University Press.

Elbow, P. (1993). Ranking, evaluating, and liking: Sorting out three forms of judgment. *College English, 55*(2), 187-206.

Fassler, B. (1978). The red pen revisited: Teaching composition through student conferences. *College English, 40*(2), 186-190.

Flower, L. (1979). Writer-based prose: A cognitive basis for problems in writing. *College English, 4,* 19-37.

Flower, L., & Hayes, J. (1981). A cognitive process theory of writing. *College Composition and Communication, 32,* 365-387.

Flynn, E. A. (1989). Learning to read student papers from a feminine perspective, I. In B. Lawson, S. S. Ryan, & W. R. Winterowd (Eds.), *Encountering student texts: Interpretive issues in reading student writing* (pp. 49-58). Urbana, IL: National Council of Teachers of English.

Flynn, J. F. (1989). Learning to read student papers from a feminine perspective, II. In B. Lawson, S. S. Ryan, & W. R. Winterowd (Eds.), *Encountering student texts: Interpretive issues in reading student writing* (pp. 131-137). Urbana, IL: National Council of Teachers of English.

Freedman, A., & Pringle, I. (1980). Writing in the college years: Some indices of growth. *College Composition and Communication, 31,* 311-324.

Freeman, C. P., & Hatch, R. A. (1975). A behavioral grading system that works. *ABCA Bulletin, 38*(2), 1-9.

Friedman, P. G. (1974). *Objectives, evaluation, and grading in interpersonal communication courses: An experiential perspective.* Paper presented at the annual meeting of the International Communication Association, New Orleans, LA. ED 091 786. 21 pp. MF–01; PC–01.

Fulwiler, T. (1986). The argument for writing across the curriculum. In A. Young & T. Fulwiler (Eds.), *Writing across the disciplines: Research into practice* (pp. 21-32). Portsmouth, NH: Heinemann.

Fulwiler, T., Gorman, M. E., & Gorman, M. E. (1986). Changing faculty attitudes toward writing. In A. Young & T. Fulwiler (Eds.), *Writing across the disciplines: Research into practice* (pp. 53-67). Portsmouth, NH: Heinemann.

Gabriel, S. L. (1990). Gender, reading, and writing: Assignments, expectations, and responses. In S. J. Gabriel & I. Smithson (Eds.), *Gender in the classroom: Power and pedagogy* (pp. 127-139). Urbana, IL: University of Illinois Press.

Gallehr, D. R. (1993). Portfolio assessment in the college writing classroom. In K. Gill (Ed.), *Process and portfolios in writing instruction* (pp. 75-80). Urbana, IL: National Council of Teachers of English.

Garrison, D. A. (1979). Measuring differences in the assigning of grades. *Improving College and University Teaching, 27*(2), 68-71.

Gibson, M. (1992). Alone and loving it. *Journal of Teaching Writing, 11*(1), 119-128.

Greenbaum, S., & Taylor, J. (1981). The recognition of usage errors by instructors of freshman composition. *College Composition and Communication, 32,* 169-174.

Hahn, J. (1981). Students' reactions to teachers' written comments. *National Writing Project Network Newsletter, 4,* 7-10.

Hairston, M. (1981). Not all errors are created equal: Nonacademic readers in the professions respond to lapses in usage. *College English, 43,* 794-806.

Hamp-Lyons, L., & Condon, W. (1993). Questioning assumptions about portfolio-based assessment. *College Composition and Communication, 44,* 176-190.

Harris, M. (1986). *Teaching one-to-one: The writing conference.* Urbana, IL: National Council of Teachers of English.

Harris, M. (1990). Teacher/student talk: The collaborative conference. In S. Hynds & D. L. Rubin (Eds.), *Perspectives on talk and learning* (pp. 149-162). Urbana, IL: National Council of Teachers of English.

Haswell, R. H. (1983). Minimal marking. *College English, 45,* 600-604.

Haswell, R. H., & Tedesco, J. E. (1991, November). *Gender and the evaluation of writing.* Paper presented at the annual meeting of the National Council of Teachers of English, Seattle, WA. ED 343 141. 14 pp. MF–01; PC–01.

Hays, J. (1978). *Play it again, Sandra: The use of tape cassettes to evaluate student compositions.* Paper presented at the annual meeting of the Conference on College Composition and Communication, Denver, CO. ED 162 332. 19 pp. MF–01; PC–01.

Heller, D. A. (1989). Silencing the soundtrack: An alternative to marginal comments. *College Composition and Communication, 40,* 210-215.

Hewitt, G. (1995). *A portfolio primer: Teaching, collecting, and assessing student writing.* Portsmouth, NH: Heinemann.

Hiatt, M. (1975). Students at bay: The myth of the conference. *College Composition and Communication, 26,* 38-41.

Hirsch, E. D., & Harrington, D. P. (1981). Measuring the communicative effectiveness of prose. In C. H. Frederiksen & J. F. Dominic (Eds.), *The nature, development, and teaching of written communication* (Vol. 2, pp. 189-207). Hillsdale, NJ: Erlbaum.

Hobson, E. H. (1998). Designing and grading written assignments.

In R. S. Anderson & B. W. Speck (Eds.), *Changing the way we grade student performance: Classroom assessment and the new learning paradigm* (pp. 51-57). New Directions for Teaching and Learning No. 74. San Francisco: Jossey-Bass.

Houston, L. (1983). Grading: The student's option. *The Technical Writing Teacher, 11*(1), 21-22.

Hovarth, B. K. (1984). The components of written response: A practical synthesis of current views. *Rhetoric Review, 2*(2), 136-156.

Howard, R. M. (1995). Plagiarisms, authorships, and the academic death penalty. *College English, 57,* 788-806.

Hudgins, R. R. (1987). Tips on teaching report writing. *Chemical Engineering Education, 21*(3), 130-132.

Hurst, C. J. (1975). Cassette grading improves student report writing. *Engineering Education, 65,* 429-430.

Keech, C. L. (1982, March). *Unexpected directions of change in student writing performance.* Paper presented at the annual conference of the American Educational Research Association, New York, NY. ED 220 538. 41 pp. MF–01; PC–02.

Kirby, S. C. (1987). Self-evaluation: A way to improve teaching and learning. *Teaching English in the Two-Year College, 14,* 41-46.

Kline, C. R., Jr. (1976). I know you think you know what I said. *College English, 37,* 661-662.

Knapp, J. W. (1976). Contract/conference evaluation of freshman composition. *College English, 37,* 647-653.

Knoblauch, C. H., and Brannon, L. (1984). *Rhetorical traditions and the teaching of writing.* Upper Montclair, NJ: Boynton/Cook.

Krupa, G. H. (1979). Primary trait scoring in the classroom. *College Composition and Communication, 30,* 214-215.

Larson, R. L. (1986). Making assignments, judging writing, and annotating papers: Some suggestions. In C. W. Bridges (Ed.), *Training the new teacher of college composition* (pp. 109-116). Urbana, IL: National Council of Teachers of English.

Lauer, J. M. (1989). Interpreting student writing. In B. Lawson, S. S. Ryan, & W. R. Winterowd (Eds.), *Encountering student texts: Interpretive issues in reading student writing* (pp. 121-128). Urbana, IL: National Council of Teachers of English.

Lawson, B., & Ryan, S. S. (1989). Introduction: Interpretive issues in student writing. In B. Lawson, S. S. Ryan, & W. R. Winterowd (Eds.), *Encountering student texts: Interpretive issues in reading student writing* (pp. vii-xvii). Urbana, IL: National Council of Teachers of English.

Leder, J. R. (1991). An echo of Genesis: An assessment of the business writing portfolio. In P. Belanoff & M. Dickson (Eds.), *Portfolios: Process and product* (pp. 123-136). Portsmouth, NH: Boynton/Cook.

Leonard, J. S., Wharton, C. E., Davis, R. M., & Harris, J. (Eds.). (1994). *Author-ity and textuality: Current views of collaborative writing*. (Locust Hill Literary Study No. 14). West Cornwall, CT: Locust Hill Press.

Lotto, E., & Smith, B. (1979). Making grading work. *College English, 41,* 423-431.

Lynch, C., & Klemans, P. (1978, October). Evaluating our evaluations. *College English, 40,* 166-180.

Mandel, B. J. (1975). Teaching without judging. In R. Ohmann & W. B. Coley (Eds.), *Ideas for English 101: Teaching writing in college* (pp. 224-234). Urbana, IL: National Council of Teachers of English.

Marshall, M. J. (1997). Marking the unmarked: Reading student diversity and preparing teachers. *College Composition and Communication, 48,* 231-248.

McDonald, W. U., Jr. (1973). Pass/no credit in beginning composition: Problem and promise. *College Composition and Communication, 24,* 409-413.

McKendy, T. F. (1990). Legitimizing peer responses: A recycling project for placement essay. *College Composition and Communication, 41,* 89-91.

Memering, W. D. (1973). Talking to students: Group conference. *College Composition and Communication, 24,* 306-307.

Metzger, E. (1978). Measuring growth in college writing. *Journal of Basic Writing, 1*(4), 71-81.

Metzger, E., & Bryant, L. (1993). Portfolio assessment: Pedagogy, power, and the student. *Teaching English in the Two-Year College, 20,* 279-288.

Meyers, G. D. (1988). Efficient, effective evaluation: Grading business communication assignments with the primary trait scoring method. *Bulletin of the Association for Business Communication, 51*(2), 18-21.

Miller, S. (1984). The student's reader is always a fiction. *Journal of Advanced Composition, 5,* 15-29.

Mitchell, F. (1994). Is there a text in this grade? The implicit messages of comments on student writing. *Issues in Writing, 6*(2), 187-195.

Morrison, G. R., & Ross, S. M. (1998). Evaluating technology-based processes and products. In R. S. Anderson & B. W. Speck (Eds.), *Changing the way we grade student performance: Classroom assessment and the new learning paradigm* (pp. 69-77). New

Directions for Teaching and Learning No. 74. San Francisco: Jossey-Bass.

Murray, P. Y. (1989). Teachers as readers, readers as teachers. In B. Lawson, S. S. Ryan, & W. R. Winterowd (Eds.), *Encountering student texts: Interpretive issues in reading student writing* (pp. 73-85). Urbana, IL: National Council of Teachers of English.

Myers, M. (1996). Sailing ships: A framework for portfolios in formative and summative systems. In R. Calfee & P. Perfumo (Eds.), *Writing portfolios in the classroom: Policy and practice, promise and peril* (pp. 149-178). Mahwah, NJ: Erlbaum.

Najimy, N. E. (Ed.). (1981). *Measure for measure: A guidebook for evaluating students' expository writing*. Urbana, IL: National Council of Teachers of English.

Newkirk, T. (1984). Direction and misdirection in peer response. *College Composition and Communication, 35,* 301-311.

Nold, E. W. (1978). *The basics of research: Evaluation of writing*. Paper presented at the annual meeting of the Modern Language Association of America, New York, NY. ED 166 713. 12 pp. MF–01; PC–01.

Nystrand, M., Cohen, A. S., & Dowling, N. M. (1993). Addressing reliability problems in the portfolio assessment of college writing. *Educational Assessment, 1*(1), 53-70.

Odell, L., & Goswami, D. (1985). *Writing in nonacademic settings.* New York: Guilford.

Olsen, G. A. (1982). Beyond evaluation: The recorded response to essays. *Teaching English in the Two-Year College, 8,* 121-123.

Patterson, J. S. (1983). Ethos and the correction of compositions. *Teaching English in the Two-Year College, 9*(3), 176-178.

Peterson, R. (1995). *The writing teacher's companion: Planning, teaching, and evaluating in the composition classroom*. Boston: Houghton Mifflin.

Polanski, V. G. (1987). *The buddy system: A step toward more reliable grading*. Paper presented at the annual meeting of the Conference for Writing Program Administrators, Logan, UT. ED 286 201. 13 pp. MF–01; PC–01.

Proffitt, E. (1977). Grading and student choice. *Freshman English News, 6*(2), 1-2.

Rachal, J. R. (1984). Community college and university instructor consistency in the evaluation of freshman English themes. *Community/Junior College Quarterly, 8*(1-4), 127-140.

Radican, L. S. (1997). Contract grades: An agreement between teachers and their students. *Alternatives to Grading Student Writing, 4,* 285-290.

Raymond, J. C. (1976). Cross-grading: An experiment in evaluating compositions. *College Composition and Communication, 27,* 52-55.

Raymond, J. C. (1982). What we don't know about the evaluation of writing. *College Composition and Communication, 33,* 399-403.

Reckase, M. D. (1993, April). *Portfolio assessment: A theoretical prediction of measurement properties.* Paper presented at the annual meeting of the American Educational Research Association, Atlanta, GA. ED 358 138. 17 pp. MF–01; PC–01.

Reed, W. M., & Burton, J. K. (1985). Effective and ineffective evaluation of essays: Perceptions of college freshmen. *Journal of Teaching Writing, 4,* 270-283.

Rose, A. (1982). Spoken versus written criticism of student writing: Some advantages of the conference method. *College Composition and Communication, 33,* 326-331.

Ruth, L., & Murphy, S. (1988). *Designing writing tasks for the assessment of writing.* Norwood, NJ: Ablex.

Sandman, J. (1993, December). Self-evaluation exit essays in freshman composition: "Now I have new weaknesses." *Teaching English in the Two-Year College,* 275-278.

Sawyer, T. M. (1975). Accountability: Or let others grade your students. *College Composition and Communication, 26,* 335-340.

Sawyer, T. M. (1976). External examiners: Separating teaching from grading. *Engineering Education, 66,* 344-346.

Scanlon, P. A., & Ford, M. P. (1998). Grading student performance in real-world settings. In R. S. Anderson & B. W. Speck (Eds.), *Changing the way we grade student performance: Classroom assessment and the new learning paradigm* (pp. 97-105). New Directions for Teaching and Learning No. 74. San Francisco: Jossey-Bass.

Schwegler, R. A. (1991). The politics of reading student papers. In R. Bullock & J. Trimbur (Eds.), *The politics of writing instruction: Postsecondary* (pp. 203-225). Portsmouth, NH: Heinemann.

Sharplin, A. D., Sharplin, W. S., & Birdsong, T. P. (1986). Knowing the market: Are writing teachers out of touch? *Journal of Education for Business, 62,* 80.

Shaughnessy, M. (1977). *Errors and expectations: A guide for the teacher of basic writing.* New York: Oxford University Press.

Sloan, G. (1977). The wacky world of theme-marking. *College Composition and Communication, 28,* 370-373.

Smart, G. (1993). Genre as common invention: A central bank's response to its executives' expectations as readers. In R. Spilka

(Ed.), *Writing in the workplace: New research perspectives* (pp. 124-140). Carbondale & Edwardsville, IL: Southern Illinois University Press.

Smith, K. A. (1998). Grading cooperative projects. In R. S. Anderson & B. W. Speck (Eds.), *Changing the way we grade student performance: Classroom assessment and the new learning paradigm* (pp. 59-67). New Directions for Teaching and Learning No. 74. San Francisco: Jossey-Bass.

Smith, S. (1997). The genre of the end comment: Conventions in teacher responses to student writing. *College Composition and Communication, 48,* 249-268.

Sneed, D. (1986). Writing teachers should be prepared for legal challenges. *Journalism Educator, 41*(3), 26-28.

Sommers, J., Black, L., Daiker, D. A., & Stygall, G. (1993). The challenge of rating portfolios: What WPAs can expect. *WPA: Writing Program Administration, 17*(1-2), 7-29.

Sommers, N. (1982). Responding to student writing. *College Composition and Communication, 33,* 148-156.

Speck, B. W. (1993). *Publication peer review: An annotated bibliography.* Westport, CT: Greenwood Press.

Speck, B. W. (1998a). *Grading student writing: An annotated bibliography.* Westport, CT: Greenwood Press.

Speck, B. W. (1998b). The teacher's role in the pluralistic classroom. *Perspectives, 28*(1), 19-43.

Speck, B. W. (1998c). Unveiling some of the mystery of professional judgment in classroom assessment. In R. S. Anderson & B. W. Speck (Eds.), *Changing the way we grade student performance: Classroom assessment and the new learning paradigm* (pp. 17-31). New Directions for Teaching and Learning No. 74. San Francisco: Jossey-Bass.

Speck, B. W., Johnson, T. R., Dice, C. P., & Heaton, L. B. (1999). *Collaborative writing: An annotated bibliography.* Westport, CT: Greenwood Press.

Speck, B. W., & Jones, T. R. (1998). Direction in the grading of writing? What the literature on the grading of writing does and doesn't tell us. In F. Zak & C. C. Weaver (Eds.), *The theory and practice of grading: Problems and possibilities* (pp. 17-29). Albany, NY: State University of New York Press.

Speck, B. W., & Porter, L. R. (1990). Annotated bibliography for teaching ethics in professional writing. *Bulletin of the Association for Business Communication, 53*(3), 36-52.

Stern, C. (1991). *Writing portfolios: A resource for teaching and assessment.* Paper presented at the annual meeting of the

Conference on College Composition and Communication, Boston, MA. ED 336 757. 14 pp. MF–01; PC–01.
Stewart, D. C. (1975). Aesthetic distance and the composition teacher. *College Composition and Communication, 26,* 238-243.
Stewart, D. C. (1980). Practical work for advanced composition students. *College Composition and Communication, 31,* 81-83.
Stine, D., & Skarzenski, D. (1979). Priorities for the business communication classroom: A survey of business and academe. *Journal of Business Communication, 16,* 15-30.
Straub, R. (1996). The concept of control in teacher response: Defining the varieties of "directive" and "facilitative" commentary. *College Composition and Communication, 47,* 223-251.
Straub, R., & Lunsford, R. F. (1995). *Twelve readers reading: Responding to college student writing.* Cresskill, NJ: Hampton Press.
Stygall, G., Black, L., Daiker, D. A., & Sommers, J. (1994). Gendered textuality: Assigning gender to portfolios. In L. Black, D. A. Daiker, J. Sommers, & G. Stygall (Eds.), *New directions in portfolio assessment: Reflective practice, critical theory, and large-scale scoring* (pp. 248-262). Portsmouth, NH: Boynton/Cook.
Tarvers, J. K. (1993). *Teaching writing: Theories and practices* (4th ed.). New York: HarperCollins.
Tebeaux, E. (1980). Grade report writing with a check sheet. *The Technical Writing Teacher, 7*(2), 66-68.
Thompson, R. F. (1981). Peer grading: Some promising advantages for composition research in the classroom. *Research in the Teaching of English, 15*(2), 172-174.
Throop, D. P., & Jameson, D. A. (1976). Behavioral grading: An approach worth trying. *ABCA Bulletin, 39*(3), 3-5.
Tritt, M. (1983). Exchange grading with a workshop approach to the teaching of writing. *English Quarterly, 16*(1), 16-19.
Walvoord, B. E. F. (1986). *Helping students write well* (2nd ed.). New York: Modern Language Association of America.
Walvoord, B. E., & Anderson, V. J. (1998). *Effective grading: A tool for learning and assessment.* San Francisco: Jossey-Bass.
Walvoord, B. E., Anderson, V. J., Breihan, J. R., McCarthy, L. P., Robison, S. M., & Sherman, A. K. (1996). Making traditional graded tests and assignments serve contemporary needs for assessment. In T. W. Banta, J. P. Lund, K. E. Black, & F. W. Oblander (Eds.), *Assessment in practice: Putting principles to work on college campuses* (pp. 278-281). San Francisco: Jossey-Bass.
Warren, T. L. (1976). Objective grading standards in technical writing. *The Technical Writing Teacher, 4*(1), 29-31.
Weaver, G. E. (1986). Just what the doctor ordered: A possible cure

for "paper-graditis." *Bulletin of the Association for Business Communication, 49*(2), 43-44.

Weeks, F. W. (1978). The meaning of grades. In G. H. Douglas (Ed.), *The teaching of business communication* (pp. 163-166). Champaign, IL: American Business Communication Association.

Welch, N. (1998). Sideshadowing teacher response. *College English, 60*(4), 374-395.

Westcott, W., & Gardner, P. (1984). Holistic scoring as a teaching device. *Teaching English in the Two-Year College, 11*(2), 35-39.

Whichard, N. W., Gamber, G., Lester, V., Leighton, G., Carlberg, J., & Whitaker, W. (1992). Life in the margin: The hidden agenda in commenting on student writing. *Journal of Teaching Writing, 11,* 51-64.

White, E. M. (1995). Response. *College Composition and Communication, 46,* 550-551.

White, E. M., Lutz, W. D., & Kamusikiri, S. (Eds.). (1996). *Assessment of writing: Politics, policies, practices.* New York: Modern Language Association of America.

Wilkinson, D. C. (1979). Evidence that others do not agree with your grading of letters. *ABCA Bulletin, 42*(3), 29-30.

Wilson, M. (1979). The grading game. *C: JET,* 12-15.

Winterowd, W. R. (1971). The radical English class: Student faces student in discourse without grades. *California English Journal, 7*(2), 27-33.

Wolcott, W., & Legg, S. M. (Eds.). (1998). *An overview of writing assessment: Theory, research, and practice.* Urbana, IL: National Council of Teachers of English.

Zak, F. (1990). Exclusively positive responses to student writing. *Journal of Basic Writing, 9*(2), 40-53.

Zak, F., & Weaver, C. C. (Eds.). (1998). *The theory and practice of grading: Problems and possibilities.* Albany, NY: State University of New York Press.

Zebroski, J. T. (1989). A hero in the classroom. In B. Lawson, S. S. Ryan, & W. R. Winterowd (Eds.), *Encountering student texts: Interpretive issues in reading student writing* (pp. 35-47). Urbana, IL: National Council of Teachers of English.

Zhu, W. (1995). Effects of training for peer response on students' comments and interaction. *Written Communication, 12,* 492-528.

Ziv, N. D. (1982). *What she thought I said: How students misperceive teachers' written comments.* Paper presented at the annual meeting of the Conference of College Composition and Communication, San Francisco, CA. ED 215 361. 9 pp. MF–01; PC–01.

INDEX

A

APA style, in writing, 18-19
audience, determining when writing, 14-18

C

cheating, 47-51
common errors, 22-23
constructing writing assignments, 11-26
contract, grading, 38-41
criteria, used to evaluate writing assignments, 24-25
critiquing writing assignments, 23-26
cryptic responses, 67-68

D

drafts, 63

E

errors, common, 22-23
essential, in writing assignment, 18-21
evaluation of writing, problems with, 3-5

F

fairness, in writing evaluation, 27-44
fairness, of professor's evaluation, 27-31
feedback, for writing revision, 61-75
- as identifier for errors, 61-63
- as justifier for the grade, 63-64
- misperceptions about, 61
- oral, 8-9
- professors' difficulty in providing effectively, 65-67
- transferred from one assignment to another, 64-65
- useful, provided by professors, 70

G

generalizability, 30-31
grading and writing processes, marriage of, 8-9
grading contract, 38-41
- sample, 38-39

grading instrument, 53-56
grading methods, 31-44
- checkmark, 40
- pass-no-pass, 40
- external evaluators, 40-41

grading process, 5 -8
grading process, ways to include students, 52-53

H

holistic scoring, 36-37

I

informed decisions, preparing students to make, 51-52

J

judgment, professional, 27-44

M

methods of grading, 31-44

O

optional, in writing assignment, 18-21

P

pass/no-pass, 40
peer and self-evaluations, teaching students to conduct, 56-58
perspectives, professors' and students' differences in, 71-72
plagiarism, 47-51
portfolios, 41-44
    definition of, 41
primary trait scoring, 34-36
    guide, 35-36
professional judgment, 27-44
professorial authorities, 45-47
purpose, determining when writing, 11-14

R

reliability, of professor's evaluation, 27-31
    sources of, 32
responses, cryptic, 67-68
    negative, 68-70
    too much of, 70
rubric for writing assignment, 54-56
    sample of, 54

S

scoring, holistic, 36-37
scoring, primary trait, 34-36

speaking comments, for revision, 72
standards, used to evaluate students' writing, 21-23
student-professor conferences, 58-59

T
terminology, used for evaluation, 4-7

V
validity, of professor's evaluation, 27-31
sources of, 32

W
writing and grading processes, marriage of, 8-9
writing comments, for revision, 72-74
sample of, 81-84
writing process, 1-3
list, use of to describe, 2-3
writing to learn, 11-14
writing to inform, 11-14

ASHE-ERIC HIGHER EDUCATION REPORTS

Since 1983, the Association for the Study of Higher Education (ASHE) and the Educational Resources Information Center (ERIC) Clearinghouse on Higher Education, a sponsored project of the Graduate School of Education and Human Development at The George Washington University, have cosponsored the ASHE-ERIC Higher Education Report series. This volume is the twenty-seventh overall and the tenth to be published by the Graduate School of Education and Human Development at The George Washington University.

Each monograph is the definitive analysis of a tough higher education problem, based on thorough research of pertinent literature and institutional experiences. Topics are identified by a national survey. Noted practitioners and scholars are then commissioned to write the reports, with experts providing critical reviews of each manuscript before publication.

Eight monographs (10 before 1985) in the ASHE-ERIC Higher Education Report series are published each year and are available on individual and subscription bases. To order, use the order form on the last page of this book.

Qualified persons interested in writing a monograph for the ASHE-ERIC Higher Education Report series are invited to submit a proposal to the National Advisory Board. As the preeminent literature review and issue analysis series in higher education, the Higher Education Reports are guaranteed wide dissemination and national exposure for accepted candidates. Execution of a monograph requires at least a minimal familiarity with the ERIC database, including *Resources in Education* and the current *Index to Journals in Education*. The objective of these reports is to bridge conventional wisdom with practical research. Prospective authors are strongly encouraged to call at (800) 773-3742.

For further information, write to
ASHE-ERIC Higher Education Report Series
The George Washington University
One Dupont Circle, Suite 630
Washington, DC 20036-1183
Or phone (202) 296-2597
Toll free: (800) 773-ERIC

Write or call for a complete catalog.

Visit our Web site at **www.eriche.org/reports**

ADVISORY BOARD

James Earl Davis
University of Delaware at Newark

Kenneth A. Feldman
State University of New York–Stony Brook

Kassie Freeman
Peabody College, Vanderbilt University

Susan Frost
Emory University

Esther E. Gottlieb
West Virginia University

Philo Hutcheson
Georgia State University

Lori White
Stanford University

CONSULTING EDITORS

Sandra Beyer
University of Texas at El Paso

Robert Boice
State University of New York–Stony Brook

Ivy E. Broder
The American University

Dennis Brown
Michigan State University

Shirley M. Clark
Oregon State System of Higher Education

Robert A. Cornesky
Cornesky and Associates, Inc.

K. Patricia Cross
Scholar in Residence

Rhonda Martin Epper
State Higher Education Executive Officers

Anne H. Frank
American Association of University Professors

Mildred Garcia
Arizona State University–West

Don Hossler
Indiana University

Dean L. Hubbard
Northwest Missouri State University

Jean E. Hunter
Duquesne University

Lisa R. Lattuca
The Spencer Foundation, Chicago, Illinois

J. Roderick Lauver
Planned Systems International, Inc.–Maryland

Daniel T. Layzell
MGT of America, Inc., Madison, Wisconsin

Barbara Lee
Rutgers University

Robert Linn
University of Chicago

Ivan B. Liss
Radford University

Anne Goodsell Love
University of Akron

Clara M. Lovett
Northern Arizona University

Meredith Ludwig
Education Statistics Services Institute

Jean MacGregor
Evergreen State College

Laurence R. Marcus
Rowan College

William McKeachie
University of Michigan

Mantha V. Mehallis
Florida Atlantic University

Robert Menges
Northwestern University

Diane E. Morrison
Centre for Curriculum, Transfer, and Technology

Barbara M. Moskal
Colorado School of Mines

John A. Muffo
Virginia Polytechnic Institute and State University

Patricia H. Murrell
University of Memphis

L. Jackson Newell
Deep Springs College

Steven G. Olswang
University of Washington

R. Eugene Rice
American Association for Higher Education

Maria Scatena
St. Mary of the Woods College

John Schuh
Iowa State University

Jack H. Schuster
Claremont Graduate School–Center for Educational Studies

Carole Schwinn
Jackson Community College

Patricia Somers
University of Arkansas at Little Rock

Leonard Springer
University of Wisconsin–Madison

Richard J. Stiggins
Assessment and Training Institute

Marilla D. Svinicki
University of Texas–Austin

David Sweet
OERI, U.S. Department of Education

Catherine S. Taylor
University of Washington

Jon E. Travis
Texas A&M University

Dan W. Wheeler
University of Nebraska–Lincoln

Christine K. Wilkinson
Arizona State University

Donald H. Wulff
University of Washington

Manta Yorke
Liverpool John Moores University

William Zeller
University of Michigan at Ann Arbor

REVIEW PANEL

Richard Alfred
University of Michigan

Thomas A. Angelo
DePaul University

Charles Bantz
Arizona State University

Robert J. Barak
Iowa State Board of Regents

Alan Bayer
Virginia Polytechnic Institute and State University

John P. Bean
Indiana University–Bloomington

John M. Braxton
Peabody College, Vanderbilt University

Ellen M. Brier
Tennessee State University

Dennis Brown
University of Kansas

Deborah Faye Carter
Indiana University

Patricia Carter
University of Michigan

John A. Centra
Syracuse University

Paul B. Chewning
Council for the Advancement and Support of Education

Arthur W. Chickering
Vermont College

Darrel A. Clowes
Virginia Polytechnic Institute and State University

Carol L. Colbeck
Pennsylvania State University

Deborah M. DiCroce
Tidewater Virginia Community College

Marty Finkelstein
Seton Hall University

Dorothy E. Finnegan
The College of William & Mary

Timothy Gallineau
Buffalo State College

Judith Glazer-Raymo
Long Island University

Kenneth C. Green
Claremont Graduate University

James C. Hearn
University of Minnesota

Donald E. Heller
University of Michigan

Edward R. Hines
Illinois State University

Deborah Hirsch
University of Massachusetts

Deborah Hunter
University of Vermont

Linda K. Johnsrud
University of Hawaii at Manoa

Bruce Anthony Jones
University of Missouri–Columbia

Elizabeth A. Jones
West Virginia University

Marsha V. Krotseng
Cleveland State University

George D. Kuh
Indiana University–Bloomington

J. Roderick Lauver
Planned Systems International, Inc.–Maryland

Daniel T. Layzell
MGT of America, Inc., Madison, Wisconsin

Ronald Lee
University of Nebraska

Patrick G. Love
Kent State University

Mantha V. Mehallis
Florida Atlantic University

Marcia Mentkowski
Alverno College

John Milam, Jr.
George Mason University

Toby Milton
Essex Community College

Christopher C. Morphew
University of Kansas

John A. Muffo
Virginia Polytechnic Institute and State University

L. Jackson Newell
Deep Springs College

Mark Oromaner
Hudson County Community College

Suzanne Ortega
University of Nebraska

James C. Palmer
Illinois State University

Michael Paulson
University of New Orleans

Robert A. Rhoads
Michigan State University

G. Jeremiah Ryan
Quincy College

Mary Ann Danowitz Sagaria
The Ohio State University

Kathleen M. Shaw
Temple University

Edward St. John
Indiana University

Scott Swail
College Bound

J. Douglas Toma
University of Missouri–Kansas City

Kathryn Nemeth Tuttle
University of Kansas

David S. Webster
Oklahoma State University

Lisa Wolf
University of Kansas

Volume 27 ASHE-ERIC Higher Education Reports

1. The Art and Science of Classroom Assessment: The Missing Part of Pedagogy
   Susan M. Brookhart
2. Due Process and Higher Education: A Systemic Approach to Fair Decision Making
   Ed Stevens

Volume 26 ASHE-ERIC Higher Education Reports

1. Faculty Workload Studies: Perspectives, Needs, and Future Directions
   Katrina A. Meyer
2. Assessing Faculty Publication Productivity: Issues of Equity
   Elizabeth G. Creamer
3. Proclaiming and Sustaining Excellence: Assessment as a Faculty Role
   Karen Maitland Schilling and Karl L. Schilling
4. Creating Learning Centered Classrooms: What Does Learning Theory Have to Say?
   Frances K. Stage, Patricia A. Muller, Jillian Kinzie, and Ada Simmons
5. The Academic Administrator and the Law: What Every Dean and Department Chair Needs to Know
   J. Douglas Toma and Richard L. Palm
6. The Powerful Potential of Learning Communities: Improving Education for the Future
   Oscar T. Lenning and Larry H. Ebbers
7. Enrollment Management for the 21st Century: Institutional Goals, Accountability, and Fiscal Responsibility
   Garlene Penn
8. Enacting Diverse Learning Environments: Improving the Climate for Racial/Ethnic Diversity in Higher Education
   Sylvia Hurtado, Jeffrey Milem, Alma Clayton-Pedersen, and Walter Allen

Volume 25 ASHE-ERIC Higher Education Reports

1. A Culture for Academic Excellence: Implementing the Quality Principles in Higher Education
   Jann E. Freed, Marie R. Klugman, and Jonathan D. Fife
2. From Discipline to Development: Rethinking Student Conduct in Higher Education
   Michael Dannells
3. Academic Controversy: Enriching College Instruction Through Intellectual Conflict
   David W. Johnson, Roger T. Johnson, and Karl A. Smith

4. Higher Education Leadership: Analyzing the Gender Gap
   Luba Chliwniak
5. The Virtual Campus: Technology and Reform in Higher Education
   Gerald C. Van Dusen
6. Early Intervention Programs: Opening the Door to Higher Education
   Robert H. Fenske, Christine A. Geranios, Jonathan E. Keller, and David E. Moore
7. The Vitality of Senior Faculty Members: Snow on the Roof—Fire in the Furnace
   Carole J. Bland and William H. Bergquist
8. A National Review of Scholastic Achievement in General Education: How Are We Doing and Why Should We Care?
   Steven J. Osterlind

Volume 24 ASHE-ERIC Higher Education Reports

1. Tenure, Promotion, and Reappointment: Legal and Administrative Implications
   Benjamin Baez and John A. Centra
2. Taking Teaching Seriously: Meeting the Challenge of Instructional Improvement
   Michael B. Paulsen and Kenneth A. Feldman
3. Empowering the Faculty: Mentoring Redirected and Renewed
   Gaye Luna and Deborah L. Cullen
4. Enhancing Student Learning: Intellectual, Social, and Emotional Integration
   Anne Goodsell Love and Patrick G. Love
5. Benchmarking in Higher Education: Adapting Best Practices to Improve Quality
   Jeffrey W. Alstete
6. Models for Improving College Teaching: A Faculty Resource
   Jon E. Travis
7. Experiential Learning in Higher Education: Linking Classroom and Community
   Jeffrey A. Cantor
8. Successful Faculty Development and Evaluation: The Complete Teaching Portfolio
   John P. Murray

Volume 23 ASHE-ERIC Higher Education Reports

1. The Advisory Committee Advantage: Creating an Effective Strategy for Programmatic Improvement
   Lee Teitel

2. Collaborative Peer Review: The Role of Faculty in Improving College Teaching
   Larry Keig and Michael D. Waggoner
3. Prices, Productivity, and Investment: Assessing Financial Strategies in Higher Education
   Edward P. St. John
4. The Development Officer in Higher Education: Toward an Understanding of the Role
   Michael J. Worth and James W. Asp II
5. Measuring Up: The Promises and Pitfalls of Performance Indicators in Higher Education
   Gerald Gaither, Brian P. Nedwek, and John E. Neal
6. A New Alliance: Continuous Quality and Classroom Effectiveness
   Mimi Wolverton
7. Redesigning Higher Education: Producing Dramatic Gains in Student Learning
   Lion F. Gardiner
8. Student Learning Outside the Classroom: Transcending Artificial Boundaries
   George D. Kuh, Katie Branch Douglas, Jon P. Lund, and Jackie Ramin-Gyurnek

ORDER FORM

27-3

Quantity **Amount**

________ Please begin my subscription to the current year's *ASHE-ERIC Higher Education Reports* at $144.00, over 25% off the cover price, starting with Report 1. ________

________ Please send a complete set of Volume ________ *ASHE-ERIC Higher Education Reports* at $144.00, over 25% off the cover price. ________

Individual reports are available for $24.00 and include the cost of shipping and handling.

SHIPPING POLICY:

- Books are sent UPS Ground or equivalent. For faster delivery, call for charges. Alaska, Hawaii, U.S. Territories, and Foreign Countries, please call for shipping information. Order will be shipped within 24 hours after receipt of request. Orders of 10 or more books, call for shipping information. All prices shown are subject to change.
- Returns: No cash refunds—credit will be applied to future orders.

PLEASE SEND ME THE FOLLOWING REPORTS:

Quantity	Volume/No.	Title	Amount
		Subtotal:	
		Less Discount:	
		Total Due:	

Please check one of the following:

☐ Check enclosed, payable to GW-ERIC.

☐ Purchase order attached.

☐ Charge my credit card indicated below:

☐ Visa ☐ MasterCard

☐☐☐☐☐☐☐☐☐☐☐☐☐☐☐☐

Expiration Date________________

Name________________________________

Title ________________ E-mail ________________

Institution________________________________

Address________________________________

City ____________ State ____________ Zip____________

Phone ____________ Fax ____________Telex____________

Signature________________________ Date____________

SEND ALL ORDERS TO:

ASHE-ERIC Higher Education Reports Series
One Dupont Cir., Ste. 630, Washington, DC 20036-1183
Phone: (202) 296-2597 ext. 13 Toll-free: (800) 773-ERIC ext. 13
FAX: (202) 452-1844
EMAIL: order@eric-he.edu

Secure on-line ordering at URL: www.eriche.org/reports

Secure on-line ordering is available:
visit our Web site at
www.eriche.org/reports

LB 1576 .S723 2000
Speck, Bruce W.
Grading students' classroom
writing